The Soldier's Friend

INDIANA HISTORICAL SOCIETY PRESS
INDIANAPOLIS 2006

The Soldier's Friend

A LIFE OF ERNIE PYLE

RAY E. BOOMHOWER

© 2006 Indiana Historical Society Press

This book is a publication of the

Indiana Historical Society Press
450 West Ohio Street
Indianapolis, Indiana 46202-3269 USA

www.indianahistory.org

Telephone orders 1-800-447-1830
Fax orders 1-317-234-0562
Online orders @ shop.indianahistory.org

Photo credit for title page: Bettmann/CORBIS

Library of Congress Cataloging-in-Publication Data

Boomhower, Ray E., 1959-
    The soldier's friend : a life of Ernie Pyle / Ray E. Boomhower.
        p. cm.
    Includes bibliographical references and index.
    ISBN-13: 978-0-87195-200-4 (alk. paper)
    ISBN-10: 0-87195-200-9 (alk. paper)
    1.   Pyle, Ernie, 1900-1945—Juvenile literature. 2. War
correspondents—United States—Biography—Juvenile literature. 3. World
War, 1939-1945—Journalists—Biography—Juvenile literature. 4. World
War, 1939-1945—Press coverage—United States—Juvenile literature. I.
Title.
    PN4874.P88B66 2006
    070.4'333092–dc22
    [B]

                                                    2006045790

Printed in the United States of America.

For Paula Corpuz, editor extraordinaire.

★

"Of course I am very sick of the war and would like to leave it and yet I know I can't. I've been part of the misery and tragedy of it for so long that I've come to feel a responsibility to it or something. I don't know quite how to put it into words, but I feel if I left it would be like a soldier deserting."

—Ernie Pyle in a letter to his wife, Jerry

Contents

Acknowledgments

★

Each August thousands of high school graduates from Indiana and around the country descend upon Bloomington to begin their college careers at Indiana University. I was one of those students in the summer of 1978.

After working on my high school newspaper, I had decided to major in journalism in college. My classes in the subject were all taken in a handsome limestone structure near the university's Indiana Memorial Union. Since 1954, the journalism building had been named in honor of one of the college's best-known students—Ernie Pyle.

During the long hours I spent in the journalism building, I tried whenever I could to visit the Ernie Pyle Lounge on the second floor, which had on display the reporter's book, typewriter, and Pulitzer Prize certificate. It was quite a reputation to live up to for any journalism student.

It has been an honor to research the life and career of the beloved World War II correspondent. Along the way, I have been helped in my work by a number of individuals. For her helpful comments on the book, I thank Charity Pollard, site manager for the Ernie Pyle State Historic Site in Dana, Indiana. I also benefited greatly from advice offered by Evelyn Hobson, for many years the curator at the Pyle site. Nobody has worked harder to ensure that Ernie's memory lives on for future generations.

For anyone writing a biography of a famous subject, there are guides who offer assistance along the way. For their help in gathering research materials on Pyle's life and times, I thank the staffs at the Pyle site and at the Lilly Library in Bloomington, Indiana.

IHS Press editors Paula Corpuz and Rachel Popma did their best to improve the book before its publication. As she has on all my previous books, my wife, Megan McKee, offered her wisdom and helpful suggestions.

Last, but certainly not least, Pat Prather at Dean Johnson Design in Indianapolis has once again used her remarkable design ability on the book.

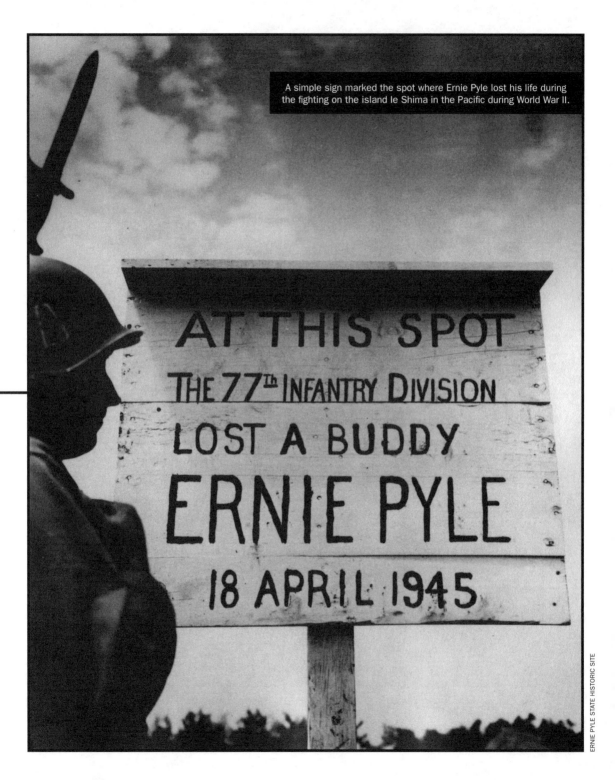

A simple sign marked the spot where Ernie Pyle lost his life during the fighting on the island Ie Shima in the Pacific during World War II.

AT THIS SPOT
THE 77ᵗʰ INFANTRY DIVISION
LOST A BUDDY
ERNIE PYLE
18 APRIL 1945

Chapter 1

The Casualty

★

In the spring of 1945, near the end of World War II, American troops landed on the island of Okinawa in the Pacific Ocean. They were there to fight against enemy soldiers from Japan, the nation that nearly four years earlier had started the war with the United States by a surprise attack on American warships at Pearl Harbor in the Hawaiian Islands.

As Japanese and American troops fought bloody battles against one another, a war correspondent new to the Pacific theater stepped ashore on Ie Shima, a small island located just west of Okinawa. On April 18, while traveling in a jeep with four American soldiers, the reporter and his companions came under fire from a Japanese soldier firing a Nambu machine gun. The men jumped from the jeep and dove for cover into a nearby ditch.

Once the firing stopped, the reporter poked his head over the top of the ditch to check on one of the soldiers, asking "Are you alright?" Another blast from the machine gun went off, hitting the journalist in the left temple, just below the rim of his helmet, killing him instantly. When found, the reporter lay where he had fallen, blood trickling from the corner of his mouth. His hands clutched the battered fatigue cap he usually wore.

Saddened by their loss, the U.S. soldiers honored their fallen friend by building a simple marker on which they wrote the following words: "At this spot, the 77th Infantry Division lost a buddy, Ernie Pyle, 18 April 1945."

To the millions of people back home in America during World War II, Ernie Pyle offered a "worm's-eye view" of the war as he reported on the life, and sometimes death, of the common soldier doing the dirty work of fighting in North Africa, Sicily, Italy, and France against the enemy forces of Nazi Germany.

At the time of Pyle's death, his writing regularly appeared in four hundred daily and three hundred weekly newspapers. He had also received journalism's highest honor—the Pulitzer Prize—in 1944 for his distinguished reporting on the war. Books of his columns had been best sellers, and one of his most famous stories, describing the death of an officer named Captain Henry T. Waskow, was made into a movie, *The Story of G.I. Joe*, starring Burgess Meredith and Robert Mitchum. In June 2002 the Hasbro toy company, maker of the famous G.I. Joe doll, released an Ernie Pyle action figure as part of its D-Day Collection.

It is quite a list of accomplishments for a boy from the small town of Dana, Indiana, whose father had been a farmer and carpenter. Pyle, however, had no plans to follow in his father's footsteps. He noted that "anything was better than looking at the south end of a horse going north." Instead of farming, Pyle turned to writing, enrolling at Indiana University in Bloomington. Journalism, he said, offered a way to escape from the backbreaking and boring labor endured by farmers. Pyle left school in 1923 to take a job as a newspaper reporter with the *LaPorte Herald* in northern Indiana.

Within a few months Pyle had accepted a better position with the *Washington Daily News* in Washington, D.C., the nation's capital. The newspaper was part of the Scripps-Howard newspaper chain. In 1926 Pyle, joined by his new wife, Geraldine "Jerry" Siebolds, quit his job to travel around the country. After working for a couple of New York newspapers, he returned to the *Daily News* and over the years worked as the newspaper's managing editor, one of the country's first aviation columnists, and a roving columnist for Scripps-Howard. He traveled across the country reporting on average people and their stories for a column that appeared in a number of

Wearing his favorite wool knit cap, Pyle works on a story for his column for the Scripps-Howard newspaper chain while covering the fighting in Europe.

newspapers six times a week. "I will go where I please and write what I please," he once said to a friend.

When America entered World War II, Pyle turned his writing skills to reporting on the experiences of U.S. fighting men overseas. The soldiers were commonly known by the nickname G.I. The letters stood for "government issue," which referred to the equipment supplied to help soldiers fight the war.

From his first reports on the fighting in North Africa to his last writing from the Pacific, Pyle slept, ate, and lived with the average soldier. Pyle at first feared meeting people, afraid they would not like him. Soldiers,

On learning of Pyle's death, President Harry Truman commented that nobody had "so well told the story" of the men fighting World War II.

4

however, instantly trusted the soft-spoken, shy, and thin man who wrote his stories about their dangerous jobs on a battered portable typewriter. They knew he always had their best interests at heart.

Although Pyle's columns covered almost every branch of the service—from those who delivered supplies by truck to pilots flying dangerous bombing missions—Pyle saved his highest praise for those who served in the infantry. "I love the infantry because they are the underdogs," he wrote. "They are the mud-rain-frost-and-wind boys. They have no comforts, and they even learn to live without the necessities. And in the end they are the guys that wars can't be won without."

John Steinbeck, a best-selling novelist and Pyle's friend, perhaps best described the reporter's work when he told *Time* magazine that there were two wars and neither had much to do with one another. There was the one war that involved maps and the movements of armies, divisions, and regiments run by high-ranking officers such as General George Marshall, chief of staff of the U.S. Army in Washington, D.C.

But there was another war, Steinbeck said. This war involved the "homesick, weary, funny, violent common men who wash their socks in their helmets, complain about the food . . . and bring themselves through as dirty a business as the world has ever seen and do it with humor and dignity and courage—and that is Ernie Pyle's war. He knows it as well as anyone and writes about it better than anyone."

As more and more people read his reports, Pyle found that his words offered comfort to family members wondering how their sons, brothers, and husbands were doing overseas. "I'm really a letter writer," he said of his work. At times, his writing also changed government policy. In a column from Italy in 1944, Pyle proposed that combat soldiers should have extra "fight pay," similar to the flight pay given to airmen. In May of that year, Congress acted on Pyle's suggestion, giving soldiers additional pay for combat service, legislation that became known as "the Ernie Pyle bill."

Other correspondents who covered the war respected Pyle and his writing. Andy Rooney, best known today for his commentary on the *60 Minutes* television program, was a young reporter covering the U.S. First Army in France during the war when he met and became friends with Pyle. One day when Rooney and other war correspondents headed to the front to look for some action, Pyle stayed behind and talked with a group of soldiers whose job it was to repair the boots of fellow G.I.s. "It wasn't a good story Ernie wrote," Rooney remembered, "it was a great story."

Despite the warmth and affection he felt for the average soldier, Pyle realized that he faced dangers in trying to report on their activities near the front lines of battle. He once wrote a friend that he tried "not to take any foolish chances, but there's just no way to play it completely safe and still do your job."

The horrors he witnessed during the war—cities turned into rubble by bombs, men torn apart by bullets and shrapnel from shells—took their toll on Pyle, who often complained of sickness. "There are days," he wrote his wife, "when you see things so horrible that you wonder what it is that can make this war worthwhile." Weary after reporting on the war in Europe, he reluctantly accepted what was to be his last assignment, covering action in the Pacific with the navy and marines.

After Pyle's death on Ie Shima, Edwin Waltz, the reporter's personal secretary while in the Pacific, discovered a column Pyle had written to be printed after the war had ended. In that column, Pyle tried to tell his readers about the awful things he had seen firsthand. He wrote that he would not soon forget "the unnatural sight of cold dead men scattered over the hillsides and in the ditches along the high rows of hedge throughout the world."

For the reader at home, Pyle said, these men were merely "columns of figures, or he is a near one who went away and didn't come back. You didn't see him lying so grotesque and pasty beside the gravel road in France." The difference, however, is that Pyle saw them, and saw them by the thousands.

Today, Pyle is remembered fondly by the generation that fought World War II as a person determined to truthfully tell the story of their service on behalf of their country. In spite of limits placed on him by wartime censors, who feared leaking secret information to the enemy, Pyle tried with his writing to inform people back home about how war had changed the G.I.s, and how they had faced extreme danger with humor, sacrifice, and bravery. As famous World War II cartoonist Bill Mauldin said when hearing of Pyle's death: "Foot soldiers have long been accustomed to losing close friends. The only difference between Ernie's death and the death of any other good guy is that the other guy is mourned by his company. Ernie is mourned by the Army."

The business district of Dana, Indiana, the small town where Pyle grew up. The scene pictured here is from the early 1940s.

Chapter 2

Growing Up in Indiana

Located just a few miles from Indiana's border with Illinois, the small Hoosier community of Dana in Vermillion County started its life in 1875 as a railroad town. Its name came from Charles Dana, editor of the *New York Sun* newspaper and a major stockholder in the Indianapolis, Decatur and Springfield Railway Company. According to local legend, the newspaper editor was so pleased about having the town named for him that he volunteered to donate books to the local library. The town had less than a thousand residents, and those who did not earn a living from the railroad often worked as farmers, planting and harvesting crops from the rich Indiana soil.

Will Pyle was one of those who tried to support his family from the land. With his wife, Maria, he worked as a hired hand on a farm west of Dana owned by Sam Elder. On August 3, 1900, Maria gave birth to their only child, a boy she named Ernest Taylor Pyle—Ernest because she liked the name, and Taylor for her maiden name. Even when their son became the world-famous columnist Ernie Pyle, Will and Maria always called him Ernest, never Ernie. (Many years later Ernie said Ernest was a name "of which I have never been overly fond.") Neighbors nicknamed the child "Shag" for his thick, light-red hair.

At a very early age, Pyle and his family moved in with Maria's sister, Mary Taylor. The house, called the Mounds, was owned by Maria and Mary's father, Lambert Taylor. The home came equipped with a party-line telephone but lacked indoor plumbing and electricity. Water for bathing and cooking had to be hauled into the home from a nearby well. A woodstove heated water for Pyle's weekly bath. Although he continued to try to earn a living as a farmer, Will Pyle never seemed at ease behind the plow. "He is a wizard

Will and Maria Pyle (back row, center) pose with a group of their neighbors in 1900. Maria's sister, Mary, is seated at the far right of the second row.

with tools, where other people are clumsy," Pyle later said of his father. "He is a carpenter at heart."

Despite his skill with tools, Will had trouble with mechanical devices, including the family car. To cure the car's brakes from squeaking, according to Pyle, his father put oil on them and then "drove to Dana and ran over the curb and through a plate-glass window and right into a dry-goods store." His son described Will as a quiet man, even with his family, who did not drink, smoke, or swear. "He has never said a great deal to me all his life," said Pyle, "and yet I feel that we have been very good friends."

Maria Pyle had quite a different personality than her husband. "My mother," Pyle noted, "would rather drive a team of horses in the field than cook a dinner." She became well known in Dana for always telling people exactly what she thought. Although her sharp tongue sometimes hurt the feelings of her neighbors, they always turned to her whenever they needed help of any kind. Young people in the area also turned to her for advice. "I don't remember her ever telling me I couldn't do something," said Pyle. "She always told me what she thought was right, and what was wrong, and then it was up to me."

A baby portrait of Ernest Taylor Pyle.

Maria's tough exterior hid a tender heart. One of Pyle's earliest memories of his childhood involved his fear of any kind of snake, from a six-inch-long garden snake to a six-foot-long rattlesnake. He recalled at the age of four or five walking behind his father as he plowed a field near a weedy fence where some wild red roses grew. Pyle asked to borrow his father's pocketknife so he could cut off some of the roses to take back home to his mother.

As Pyle sat down to gather the roses, he saw a snake—"a blue racer"—coming toward him through the grass. "I screamed, threw away the knife, and ran as fast as I could," he said. Remembering he had dropped the pocketknife, however, Pyle went back, found the knife, returned it to his father, and started to walk back home.

On the west side of the Pyles' house was an old garden filled with weeds. Afraid of seeing another snake, Pyle shouted for help to his mother. "When she came out to see what I wanted," he said, "I asked her to come and get me. She said I should come on through by myself." The scared boy began to cry, causing his mother to tell him she would whip him if he did not stop. Pyle could not stop crying or come through the garden, so his mother came, got him, and gave him one of the only two whippings he ever received from her.

When Pyle's father returned from the fields that evening, Maria told him about "the crazy boy" who had refused to walk through the weeds and had been whipped for his misbehavior. Will then told his wife about the roses and the snake. "It was the roses, I think," Pyle recalled, "that hurt her so." Ashamed of herself, Maria cried for a long time as she lay in bed that night. Many years later, tears would still come to her eyes when Ernie's mother remembered that day.

Another family member also played an important role in Ernie's life. Mary Taylor, Maria's older sister, lived with the Pyle family until her marriage to a local farmer, George Bales. Pyle described his Uncle George as a "dreamer" who would rather spend time in his garden and study the seed catalogs he had sent away for than do any actual farming. "Aunt Mary had to make the living," Pyle said. The "tall and straight" woman with "more energy than a buzz saw" worked from early in the morning to late at night raising chickens, hogs, and cattle. She also found time to attend weekly club meetings and run the local country church.

Life on the small farm located a few miles outside of Dana left its mark on Pyle, who never "felt completely at ease" in his hometown. In 1906 he started school in Dana, traveling to his class with other students in a horse and buggy driven by their teacher. Always shy, the quiet Pyle kept to himself, staying away from the rough-and-tumble games the oth-

ERNIE PYLE STATE HISTORIC SITE

Four-year-old Ernie rides a wooden hobby horse his parents ordered from the Montgomery Ward catalog.

Ernie Pyle, standing at the far right of the second row, poses with the rest of his classmates at the Bono school he attended. Pyle's best friend at the time, Thad Hooker, is standing at the far right of the first row.

er children played. "I always sat under a tree and ate my apple," he said. Pyle felt inferior to the kids from town, who could "make you feel awfully backward when you're young and a farm boy." Later, whenever he came back to Dana, he imagined that while walking down the street the town boys were still there making fun of him behind his back.

Part of Pyle's shyness may have come from his voice, which was high pitched and often cracked when he tried to talk. To make sure that this would not happen, he developed a lifelong habit of clearing his throat before he spoke. Pyle called it his "no-squeak insurance."

Although he often kept to himself, Pyle was never at a loss for companionship. He played with his cousins, the six children of his aunt and uncle, Frankie and Oat Saxton. A nearby creek offered a good spot to fish and explore, and Pyle often walked there barefoot to try his luck.

He always remembered one of the biggest fish he ever caught came to him by accident. Although the water in the creek was too muddy for swimming, Ernie and other boys would "mud crawl" by lying down and walking along on their hands and kicking with their feet. One time a fish swam inside Ernie's clothes and got caught. "It was round and blue, about a foot long—the biggest fish we had ever caught in that creek," he said. "I took it home and we had it for supper."

Pyle's closest companion in Dana was a boy a year older than himself named Thad Hooker. The two of them lived only a mile apart and believed the "world would end if we didn't see each other every day," Pyle said. Throughout their friendship, Hooker could never remember the two boys arguing or yelling at each other.

For fun, the boys imagined they were knights of King Arthur's Round Table. Using poles for spears and the lids from their mothers' wash boilers for shields, they would joust one another, Pyle on his small horse and Hooker on his black-and-white Shetland pony. Later, they became interested in trapping and sent away for information on how to bait traps and how to skin such small animals as muskrats and skunks.

The two friends did have different tastes when it came to sports. Although Hooker enjoyed playing baseball and basketball, Pyle declined to participate in such activities, due in part to his skinny body. Hooker attempted to persuade his friend to play, but he said it usually ended with Pyle saying, "Ah hell, you know I'm not good at games." Instead, Pyle read and dreamed of traveling to places far away from Dana.

On one occasion, Pyle, Hooker, and another friend, Carl Crane, attended a circus performance at Clinton, Indiana. The boys were particularly impressed by the antics of a bareback rider during the show. Once back home, Crane and Hooker were able to imitate the daredevil stunts on their horses. When Pyle tried the same trick, however, his foot caught in the stirrup and he flipped over onto his head. The horse's thundering hooves barely missed striking Ernie's head. "That ended our circus," said Crane.

As Pyle and Hooker grew older, they turned to more adult activities, including dating and learning how to smoke. At first, the boys smoked cigarettes made from corn silk. Later, they used corncob pipes with real tobacco. They smoked on the way

ERNIE PYLE STATE HISTORIC SITE

Pyle sits on the porch of his family's home, the Mounds, along with his parents and dog, Shep. Pyle wrote that Shep had been his "constant companion" during his childhood.

Dressed in overalls, the twelve-year-old Pyle never enjoyed working on the farm. Instead, he dreamed of traveling far from home.

home from school and hid their pipes inside a woodpecker hole drilled in a fence post or in rabbit holes along the roadside. Finally, Pyle forgot and left his pipe lying on a windowsill at home when he went to school one day. When he returned home, his mother handed him the pipe and said, "I see you're smoking now." Pyle said yes and that was the last he heard of it from Maria.

Pyle depended on Hooker, who had more nerve than he did, to introduce him to dating. Thad asked two girls to go out with the boys on a Sunday night. Pyle wanted to back out on the date, but his mother made him go. It took him all afternoon to dress for his date in his new brown suit. Fighting a heavy rain, the boys hitched Hooker's Shetland pony to a wagon and drove five miles to the girls' house. "They were as scared as we were," said Pyle.

For their dates, the boys and girls went to church, and Pyle and Hooker had to jump off the wagon to drag it out of the mud when they became stuck. Returning to the girls' home, the group played a game for a while. "After that the whole thing bogged down," Pyle noted.

Although the boys wanted to go home, they could not think of anything

Will and Maria Pyle stand by the family's car, a Ford.

to say to get them out the door. Finally, about midnight, one of the girls' mothers called her daughter to the other room and gave her an alarm clock. The girl took the clock into the room and held it up. "We said something about not knowing it was so late, and rushed out," Pyle remembered.

Like many youngsters who grew up on small farms in the 1900s, Pyle was expected to help with chores and even do some of the heavy plowing. "I worked like a horse from the time I was nine," Pyle recalled. The first time he ever went to work in the field his mother left the house for a club meeting. She returned, however, in the middle of the afternoon and brought her son a lunch of bread and butter and sugar. "I suppose, too," he said, "that she wanted to make sure I hadn't been dragged to death under the harrow."

An intelligent boy, Pyle tried to escape the hard and boring work on the farm by reading newspapers and

17

Pyle at age sixteen. During the summer months, he earned money by working at a variety of jobs, including helping build a railroad track for a coal company.

pasting postcards into scrapbooks. He particularly remembered summer days resting under the shade of a tree at noon for a half hour before returning to his plow (he had been up working since four in the morning). The strong summer wind steadily whipping through the trees seemed to him to be one of the "most melancholy things in all life."

Using his imagination, Pyle could see the wind continuing to blow in his face and the "faces of the little men" who would follow him on the farm until the end of time. "Horses were too slow for Ernest," said his father. "He always said the world was too big for him to be doing confining work here on the farm."

Pyle treasured the times he could leave Dana for the excitement offered by attractions in other cities, including a visit to Terre Haute with his Aunt Mary to see a performance of the Ringling Brothers' circus. He might have begun to think about becoming a reporter while on a trip to Chicago with his father. Pyle remembered being impressed by "the pictures and names of the writers, and the colored pictures of the comic-strip heroes" he saw in the *Chicago Herald-Examiner* newspaper.

A technological marvel of that time period, the automobile, offered Pyle another escape from the boring work he did on the farm. The black, drab Model T mass-produced by Henry Ford on his Detroit, Michigan, assembly lines starting in 1913 had finally offered the average American a way to escape from small-town life and see something of the world. At the age of sixteen, Pyle, thanks to his father, owned a Model T roadster. Taking Hooker and two other boys to a skating rink, Pyle crashed his car into a wagon. His father "never said a word" about the accident.

Pyle's heroes were the daredevil drivers who participated in the annual five-hundred-mile race each Memorial Day weekend at the Indianapolis Motor Speedway. First run in 1911, the Indianapolis 500 pitted man and machine in a race around the two-and-a-half mile oval paved with millions of ten-pound bricks. Pyle managed to see what became known as "the greatest spectacle in racing" in person several times and later in life listened to radio broadcasts if he could not attend. "I would rather win that race than anything in the world," he said. "I would rather be Ralph DePalma [an Indianapolis 500 driver] than President."

Pyle's graduation photograph from Bono High School. The commencement program misspelled his name as "Pyles."

As Pyle prepared to graduate from the consolidated high school at nearby Bono, Indiana, in 1918, he faced an uncertain future. Just the year before, President Woodrow Wilson had made the difficult decision to involve America in the war that had been raging in Europe since 1914. America had tried to be neutral in the fighting that broke out between Germany and Austria-Hungary (the Central Powers) against England, France, and Russia (the Allies). The sinking of American ships carrying goods to England by German submarines had finally prompted Wilson to ask Congress on April 2, 1917, for a declaration of war against the Central Powers.

Like thousands of other young men around the country, Ernie's friend Hooker left his small-town life and volunteered for service in the army to, in Wilson's words, "make the world safe for democracy." Hooker often sent Pyle postcards from the army camp in

19

Pyle's parents proudly pose for a photo on the day of their only son's graduation from high school.

Texas where he had been sent for training. At commencement exercises in the spring of 1918 for Ernie's graduation from high school, an empty, flag-draped chair was placed on the stage in Hooker's honor. "I could hardly go to commencement," Pyle said, "I was so ashamed that I wasn't in the Army, too."

Just a few weeks after his graduation, Pyle left Dana for Peoria, Illinois, where he enrolled in the U.S. Naval Reserve. The government sent him to the University of Illinois for training. Once there, Pyle wrote his parents that he and another boy had wandered into town and had "sat in front of the depot . . . and watched the trains go by. He likes trains as well as I do, and we sat and talked about how we would like to be on one of the engines firing." Pyle hoped to serve his country and see the world, but shortly before he was to be sent for additional training to the Great Lakes Naval Training Station in Chicago, the war ended.

Returning to Dana, Pyle searched for a way to escape life on the farm. "He always had big ideas," remembered Nellie Kuhns Hendrix, a neighbor. "He wanted to do things." In the fall of 1919 Ernie enrolled in college at Indiana University in Bloomington, located approximately ninety miles south of his hometown.

Life at the Bloomington campus was rough at first for the small-town freshman. Pyle had hoped to join one of the fraternities on campus. Kappa Sigma had expressed interest in having him join and invited him to a party. The fraternity members changed their minds, however, and failed to let him know of their decision. Pyle sat on the porch of the rooming house where he lived waiting for a ride to the party that never came.

Pyle soon, however, made two important friends that helped to set him on the road to fame as a journalist. One was Paige Cavanaugh, a native of Salem, Indiana, who had served two years in France with the American army. The freshmen developed a friendship that lasted the rest of their lives, with the men visiting and writing each other whenever they could. "We enjoyed each other's company," said Cavanaugh. "We had a common background. Ernie was always good conversation whether he was being silly or serious."

According to Cavanaugh, Pyle, during his early days at the university, suffered from a bad case of hero worship. The enrollment at IU had increased sharply to approximately three thousand students with the return of soldiers from the war. Although Pyle and his new friend had "a good eye for phonies around the campus," said Cavanaugh, nobody who had served overseas in the war "could do wrong in Ernie's eyes, no matter how big a blowhard he was."

Pyle also continued to admire race car drivers, trying to get Cavanaugh to attend the Indianapolis 500 with him. Ernie hoped they could get close to one of the drivers and convince him to hire one of them as a mechanic.

Another important person in Pyle's life in Bloomington had a high-ranking job at IU. Clarence E. Edmondson served as dean of men for the university. Every year, Edmondson interviewed freshman students, asking them about their hobbies and plans for the future. The shy Pyle became friends with the dean and his wife, visiting the couple at their home for long talks.

"They were never deans to me, even in the old days," Pyle wrote later in one of his columns. "They were people. We were friends, and I believe they taught me more of what life is about than anybody else in my youth, except my parents."

According to Cavanaugh and Edmondson, each played a role in pointing Pyle to a career as a newspaper reporter. During his interview with Pyle, the dean learned that the freshman had an interest in studying journalism. At that time, IU did not offer a degree in journalism, so Pyle majored in economics instead. Cavanaugh said he urged his friend to join him in taking journalism classes as a sophomore because they were supposed to be easy.

Pyle later said that journalism offered him "an escape from a farm life and farm animals." He and Cavanaugh walked into a journalism class together. When the professor finally looked up and saw them, Pyle, after clearing his throat, simply said: "We aspire to become journalists, sir."

As a sophomore Pyle, with the help of a friend, Walter B. "Shorty" Lang, another war veteran and a friend from Dana, joined Sigma Alpha Epsilon and lived in the fraternity's house. He attended dances and sometimes gathered with Cavanaugh and other students to eat sandwiches and drink Cokes at the Book Nook restaurant on Indiana Avenue. While there, he might have heard another student, Hoagy Carmichael, playing the piano and working on his legendary song "Stardust."

During the second semester of his sophomore year, Pyle began working on the student newspaper, the *Indiana Daily Student*. Those students studying journalism were responsible for writing and editing articles that appeared in the newspaper. Pyle, called "Red" for his red hair by those who worked on the paper, also served in the important positions of city editor and news editor.

John E. Stempel, who also worked on the *Daily Student* and later became head of the IU journalism department, remembered that Pyle had a "keen news sense, but his editors often complained of the utter simplicity of his writings." Stempel also said Pyle seemed shy, but tried to cover it up "with a hard-boiled manner."

One night while he worked at the *Daily Student* Ernie heard a story that had a great effect on his future work as a reporter. As part of his job, Pyle received by telephone reports from the Associated Press bureau in Indianapolis that he had to write up on a typewriter.

One of the reports Ernie worked on in November 1921 involved a series of articles by Kirke Simpson telling of the burial of the Unknown Soldier from World War I at Arlington National Cemetery in Washington, D.C. The dispatches, for which Simpson received the Pulitzer Prize, were so moving that they brought tears to Pyle's eyes and gave him a goal for his writing. Many years later, he could still quote parts of the articles that Simpson had penned.

Being on the student newspaper offered Pyle a chance to realize his childhood dreams of travel, especially when it came to sports. "You could count on seeing him at every athletic event, covering it for the *Daily Student*," said Earl Keisker, a Richmond, Indiana, native who sat alongside Pyle in one journalism class.

Although often lacking money, Pyle always seemed to find ways to make it to out-of-town games. When the IU football team traveled to Cambridge, Massachusetts, to play Harvard University, Pyle switched jobs with the *Daily Student*'s sports editor, and he and several other students pooled their money to buy a beat-up car to drive to the game. The car, however, caught fire in Boston, and Pyle had to hitchhike home.

Pyle's greatest adventure as a student came in the spring of 1922 when IU's twelve-man baseball squad made plans to travel to Japan to play a series of ten games against Waseda University and other teams. "I've got to go!" Pyle told his friend Cavanaugh. Pyle went and talked about his plans with Dean Edmondson, who, along with his wife, joined the baseball team

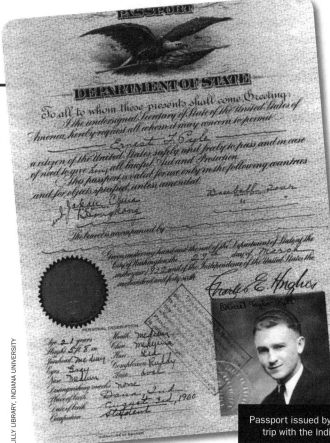

Passport issued by the U.S. State Department to Pyle for his trip with the Indiana University baseball team to Japan.

on the trip. Edmondson gave his permission, and Pyle and three of his fraternity brothers—Harold Kaiser, Joe Benham, and Warren Cooper—found jobs on the *Keystone State*, the ship that took the baseball team to Japan. "I am in perfect health, and I think I have a pretty level head, so there is not the slightest cause to worry about me," Pyle wrote his parents as the ship sailed from Seattle, Washington, across the Pacific Ocean to Japan.

During the voyage, Pyle worked as a bellboy. He earned $30 a month by seeing to the many requests from the passengers on board for such services as shining shoes, delivering packages, and fixing bathtubs. Pyle wrote about his experiences, including a bout of seasickness, in an article he mailed to the *Daily Student*. The story became the first one for which he received credit by name in the newspaper. In the article he noted that after five days at sea the ship came upon a storm that many of the crew said "was the worst they had ever seen on the Pacific with the exception of a typhoon."

One of Pyle's worst moments during the trip was likely due to the rough seas. During the 1920s, the American government had passed a law that banned the manufacture and sale of alcohol. The *Keystone State*, however, had docked in Canada where "a great many very suspicious cases were swung aboard," Edmondson noted. The cabin boys, including Pyle, rushed around balancing trays filled with bottles and glasses. Once Pyle lost his balance and spilled something on a passenger, who yelled at him. He never forgot the incident.

Thankfully, Pyle and his fraternity friends were usually treated well by the ship's passengers and officers. In a letter to his parents, Pyle noted that one of the ship's officers told him that he wished every member of the crew did their work as well as he had. Edmondson, however, worried that the boys were not getting enough fruits and vegetables to eat when they dined with the rest of the crew members. He asked each member of the baseball team to bring from the dining room "an apple or orange or some other bit of fruit after dinner to my cabin where Pyle came each evening to collect 'the loot,'" Edmondson recalled.

When the ship arrived in Japan, Pyle and his friends had to remain on board to finish their duties for the rest of the voyage. They missed seeing the baseball team play, but did have the chance to tour some Japanese cities before the ship set sail for China and the Philippines. The boys were able to purchase souvenirs, including pearl necklaces, carved ivory cigarette holders and pipes, and Japanese art prints. Upon his return home, Pyle gave some of his souvenirs to friends and sold others.

The *Keystone State* returned to Japan to pick up the IU team for the return home. "Ernie was now a veteran," said Edmondson, "and carried his tray 'with the greatest of ease.'" When the ship docked once again in Seattle, Pyle and his fraternity brothers walked off with a new friend, a stowaway from the Philippines named Eugene Uebelhardt whom they had successfully hid on the ship. Pyle took Uebelhardt with him to Dana to meet his parents and introduced his friend to them as "the boy I brought back from the Philippines."

Returning to Bloomington, Pyle arranged a job for Uebelhardt at his fraternity house and helped him to enroll at the local high school. Pyle became editor-in-chief of the *Daily Student* for the university's summer session. The newspaper appeared two days a week, every Tuesday and Friday. He also became editor of a new edition of the *Daily Student* handed out to those attending the annual Indiana State Fair in Indianapolis. That fall, his senior year, Pyle continued to work on the newspaper and the campus yearbook, the *Arbutus*, as well as joining a number of influential campus organizations.

The boy who had not been good at sports growing up in Dana also earned a varsity letter as manager of the football team. Pyle's work with the team came about as the result of a new system tried by the university to create closer cooperation between the athletic department and students. Pyle was even called upon to give a speech at a pep

A photograph of Pyle taken during his senior year at Indiana University in Bloomington, Indiana.

rally attended by thousands of other students. During his talk, with one of his arms extended to make a point, he spotted one of his friends in the crowd laughing at him. "I went completely blank," Pyle remembered. "I finally walked off the stage, with my arm sticking out. Everybody howled." He promised himself that would be the last speech he ever made.

Pyle did not finish his senior year at the university. Joseph W. Piercy, then head of the journalism department, received a letter from Charles A. Beal, editor of the *LaPorte Herald*. Beal asked Piercy if he could recommend someone for a job opening on the northern Indiana newspaper. "We needed a reporter badly," Beal recalled. Piercy immediately thought of Pyle and recommended him to Beal in "glowing terms."

With his parents urging him to stay in school and receive his degree, Pyle went for advice to his friend Edmondson. Although Pyle had no trouble with his other courses while at IU, Edmondson noted that the student's grades indicated to him that journalism was his true calling. The dean advised Pyle to take the job, which he did. He also may have been pushed to leave by heartbreak. A girl he had been dating at the university, Harriet Davidson, had recently ended their romance. At the age of twenty-two, Pyle left to begin his career as a professional reporter.

Joining Pyle (far left) in the littered newsroom at the *Washington Daily News* are (left to right) Charles Egan, Lee Miller, "June" Thornton, Paul McCrea, and John M. Gleissner, who served as editor.

Chapter 3

The Reporter

★

Life on a small-town newspaper proved to be hard at first for Ernie Pyle. He started work at the *LaPorte Herald* on January 28, 1923. Young reporters like Pyle were given the jobs nobody else wanted and were often teased by those with much more experience in journalism. The newspaper's editors did not think much of their new employee, who earned a salary of $25 per week. Ray E. Smith, city editor for the *Herald*, said both he and editor Charles Beal thought they "had picked a lemon," as Pyle did not look like a reporter with his bashful behavior and bushy red hair.

Finding a room at the local Young Men's Christian Association (YMCA), Pyle set to work covering assignments involving the courthouse, the police station, and city hall. He soon won the respect of his fellow journalists. "He made friends easily, was conscientious, and a good writer," Beal remembered. "We in the office knew he was going places." Despite the praise,

Ernie remained modest, never letting anybody on the *Herald* forget that he was "a country boy" and a "poor devil."

Early in his work at the Indiana newspaper, Pyle received an assignment from Smith to cover an important story involving an organization making news in the Hoosier State. During the 1920s the Ku Klux Klan, a racist group that had its start in the South following the Civil War, developed into a powerful force in Indiana.

In small towns, large cities, and rural areas throughout the Hoosier State, the Klan recruited members to wear its white robes and listen to its message of hate against people it did not like. These included such religious and ethnic groups as Roman Catholics, Jews, African Americans, and Eastern Europeans. Through its leader, D. C. Stephenson, the Klan dominated Indiana politics, throwing its support behind a variety of candidates for local and state offices.

Smith had heard rumors that the Klan would be sponsoring a membership recruitment meeting in LaPorte. Because Pyle was new in town and few, if any, knew that he worked at the newspaper, Smith assigned him to attend the meeting and to report on what he saw. Some of the men attending the Klan gathering grew suspicious of the stranger, however, and followed Pyle back to the YMCA. The men came into Pyle's room, questioned him about what he was doing, and warned him not to write anything about what had gone on at the meeting. Despite the threat, Pyle wrote his article and had it published in the *Herald* without any problems.

Just three months into his new job at the newspaper, Pyle received a raise to $27.50 per week. He did not remain long in LaPorte, however, as a newspaper that had just begun publishing in Washington, D.C., the *Washington Daily News*, offered him a chance to join its staff. Pyle had been recommended for the job by a friend, Nelson Poynter, then editor of the *Indiana Daily Student* and later a leading American journalist. Poynter had talked about Pyle with Earle E. Martin, editor of the *Daily News*, who was looking to hire "bright young men" for his newspaper, owned by the powerful Scripps-Howard company.

Pyle accepted Martin's offer of $30 a week to work in the nation's capital, joining a staff that included Poynter for a time, fellow Hoosier Emerson "Abe" Martin, and a young reporter named Lee Miller. Miller and Pyle became close friends. According to Miller, the staff at the tabloid-style newspaper worked hard at their jobs and developed a real fondness for the *Daily News*. "We didn't make much money," said Miller, "but we had a lot of fun."

The *Daily News* shared newsroom space at its five-story Washington, D.C., office on New York Avenue with a United Press bureau. Pyle can be seen at his desk at the far right of the photo.

When the last edition of the paper had been printed, the reporters would push their desks together and play cards, usually poker or blackjack, which Pyle preferred. Often as they played, the reporters passed around a half-gallon Mason jar filled with gin. No matter how much he may have drunk the night before, Pyle, said Miller, could always be counted on to report for work bright and early the next morning. The other reporters insisted they could not start the day without Pyle's morning routine—a loud belch that echoed throughout the newsroom.

After first working as a reporter, Pyle moved to the copy desk. There, he wrote headlines and turned long, boring stories into short, interesting pieces for the next day's edition. "He was never one to spend half a dozen words on an idea when one little active verb would handle it," Abe Martin said of Pyle. Martin also noted that every once in a while the bosses at the *Daily News* would post Pyle's work on a bulletin board as an example the rest of the staff should follow.

While working on the copy desk, Pyle displayed characteristics that lasted the rest of his career. He could not stand cold temperatures and complained frequently about being ill. Whenever he was asked by other staff members how he felt, Pyle responded with a one-word answer: "Terrible!" To ward off the chill, he took to wearing warm clothes.

Pyle seldom cared about whether or not he seemed to be well dressed to others. He preferred to wear comfortable outfits that sometimes included a simple lumberjack shirt and a long stocking cap. Roy W. Howard, Scripps-Howard president, came to the newsroom one day and spotted Pyle wearing his odd clothing. Howard turned to an editor and asked: "What's *that*?"

In the fall of 1923, Pyle received an invitation from Anita Hanna, a friend from Indiana University, to a dinner party at her house. Joining the party was Hanna's roommate, a young woman from Langdon, Minnesota, named Geraldine "Jerry" Siebolds. Before Siebolds and Pyle could talk, however, Pyle had to leave to cover a community Halloween event. It would be another year before the two started a romance that led to marriage.

Siebolds had come to Washington, D.C., during World War I. She worked as a clerk for the Civil Service Commission, enjoyed reading poetry, and considered herself to be a free spirit. Once Miller and Pyle went to Siebolds's apartment for dinner only to discover that the local electric company had turned off service to the apartment, leaving it without power. Refusing to compromise with the company, Siebolds used candles to provide enough light to eat by.

When it came to marrying Pyle in July 1925, Siebolds again displayed the nonconformity she was known for by her friends. She agreed to marry Pyle, but wanted to keep the fact a secret from their friends in Washington, D.C. She also refused to wear a wedding ring. The newlyweds eventually lived in a small Connecticut Avenue apartment with one large room and only a few pieces of furniture. Pyle and his new wife both rolled their own cigarettes, and stray bits of tobacco were scattered across the floor "like sawdust in an old saloon," noted Miller.

Marriage did not curb Pyle's desire to travel. Growing tired of his work on the copy desk at the *Daily News*, he convinced his wife that they should quit their jobs, use their $1,000 in savings, and hit the open road. Pyle bought a Ford Model T roadster automobile, a tent, and camping equipment, and set off in June 1926 to drive around the rim of the United States. After driving all day, the Pyles would camp by the roadside at night. "We both cooked," said Jerry, "but Ernie was more experienced than I."

After driving through the southern states, the Pyles headed to the American southwest before visiting Ernie's good friend Paige Cavanaugh in Los Angeles, California. The couple bumped into trouble as they traveled through the Pacific Northwest. Someone had thrown tacks onto the road, and Ernie had to deal with nineteen tire changes in one morning.

After traveling for ten weeks and putting nine thousand miles on their Ford automobile, the Pyles found themselves stopped for the night in Elizabeth, New Jersey. That night, a thunderstorm blew down their tent. The

(Left) In 1926 Pyle and his wife, Jerry, combined their savings and set out to drive around the United States. They wore simple, white outfits on their trip.

(Above) Pyle takes a break in central Washington during his trip around the country with his wife. The Ford automobile the couple used is packed with the camping equipment and supplies they needed for their journey.

Pyles were so tired that they let the rain soak their clothes. The next morning, they drove into New York City "in a downpouring rain, on two cylinders, with knots as big as teakettles on all four tires," said Pyle. He had to sell the car in order to have enough money to get something to eat.

Settling in New York with Jerry, Pyle found work on two New York newspapers, the *Evening World* and the *Post*. During his days at the *Post*, Pyle became known for his skill in writing headlines for news stories. The staff at the newspaper particularly enjoyed a headline Pyle came up with for an article about a driver who lost a fight to robbers who stole his car and drove away, leaving the victim at the side of the road. Pyle's headline read: "Thieves Rob Man, Throw Him Away."

At Pyle's old newspaper, the *Washington Daily News*, Miller had taken over as managing editor. "We were shorthanded, as usual," Miller said, "and badly needed a good telegraph editor." To fill the job of handling news copy sent by telegraph to the *Daily News*, Miller turned to his friend Pyle, offering him $60 a week. Pyle accepted on the condition that Miller remain as managing editor. Officials at the newspaper agreed to Pyle's terms, and on Christmas Eve 1927, he and Jerry returned to Washington.

After only a few months into his eight-hour-a-day assignment as telegraph editor, Pyle became restless. One day he asked Miller if he could, as a side job, write a column on aviation for the *Daily News*. Today, the period between World War I and World War II is often described as the golden age of the airplane in the United States. Pilots who had served in the air corps in France had returned to America as heroes. They continued to show off their skills by barnstorming across the country, offering rides in their rickety aircraft and performing dangerous stunts in thrilling air shows.

Editors at the *Daily News* realized that Pyle had a good idea. They remembered the excitement caused by Charles A. Lindbergh's historic May 20, 1927, nonstop solo flight across the Atlantic Ocean onboard the *Spirit of St. Louis*. Other pilots, famous names such as Amelia Earhart, Wiley Post, Richard Bird, and Howard Hughes, had followed in Lindbergh's wake, attempting to break records in this new venture. On March 26, 1928, Pyle began one of the nation's first columns devoted to aviation.

Pyle developed a regular routine to fill his column in its early days. After finishing his work as telegraph editor in the afternoon, he traveled by streetcar or taxi to the Washington area's numerous private and military airports to gather information for his column. He talked to pilots, mechanics, government officials, and anyone involved in aviation with a story to tell.

Although he never learned to fly, Pyle spent much time in the air during his days as aviation columnist for the *Daily News*.

With Much Love, Ernest

Xmas. 1928.

33

Amelia Earhart, the first woman to fly solo across the Atlantic Ocean, praised Pyle for his work on behalf of aviation during the 1920s. Earhart vanished during an around-the-world flight in 1937.

Although he never learned to fly, Pyle had plenty of experience in the air, flying approximately 100,000 miles as a passenger during the more than four years he wrote his column. His dedication to his job won the trust of those he interviewed, and his apartment became a favorite gathering spot for pilots and their friends.

The friendships he developed brought Pyle plenty of news for his column, particularly from the daredevil pilots who flew airplanes carrying the U.S. mail. On one occasion, a pilot on a newly established air-mail service from New York to Atlanta experienced trouble with his plane and had to bail out, parachuting safely to the ground. The pilot's first telephone call was to postal officials; his second call was to Pyle.

Pyle even earned a reputation as a good-luck charm of sorts for pilots attempting dangerous feats. When a young naval lieutenant, Apollo Soucek, completed a flight setting a new altitude record, Pyle was there to congratulate him and hand him a post-flight cigarette. The same routine occurred on

Soucek's second flight. Upon the completion of his third flight at the Naval Air Station, however, Soucek noticed that Pyle was not there to hand him his traditional cigarette. The pilot refused to smoke until the reporter could be located. Pyle, working across the Potomac River at the Washington-Hoover Airport, heard about the request, caught a ride with a taxi, and finally gave the pilot his cigarette.

The aviation feature became such a hit with readers that *Daily News* officials released Pyle from his duties as telegraph editor and gave him the opportunity to write his column full time. In addition to typical hard news on legislation and crashes, he began to include more human-interest items in his column, developing the style he later became famous for reporting on World War II. These personal stories included the tale of Hard Luck Bates, a passenger who had survived five crashes in two years without a scratch, as well as a mail pilot who fell two thousand feet before finding the ripcord to his parachute.

Through his column, Pyle became an influential figure in the world of flying, earning the title of aviation editor for the Scripps-Howard newspaper chain. Pyle's fame grew to such an extent that when a newspaper editor attempted to introduce the famous aviatrix Earhart to Pyle, the female flier said: "Not to know Ernie Pyle is to admit that you yourself are unknown in aviation."

Visiting Pyle in Washington after not seeing him for a couple of years, Cavanugh noticed that his friend's apartment had become a busy place, with pilots dropping by for visits at odd hours and the telephone ringing constantly. Cavanaugh went with Pyle when he visited airports and government offices charged with keeping track of the growing aviation industry. "I was terrifically impressed with all these big people being so nice and friendly to Ernie," said Cavanaugh. "They

Pyle became friends with pilots from all over the world thanks to his aviation column. Here he visits with a group at Hoover Field in Washington, D.C., in September 1928. From left to right are: Pyle; Hans Lubig, a German flyer; Hugh Wells, a test pilot; Russell Lwen, a *New York Times* reporter; Clarence Chamberlin, a pilot; Clem Gerson, manager of the Carlton Hotel in Washington; and an unnamed Gerson assistant.

didn't put up any false fronts with him." The grueling pace took its toll on Pyle, however, as Cavanaugh noted that his friend, only twenty-seven years old at the time, "looked like an old man."

AnnieBelle DePriest Moreton, a stewardess for Eastern Air Lines, remembered meeting Pyle on a flight to New York. When bad weather hit the plane, Pyle tried to comfort a nervous Moreton. "It never seemed the least bit odd," she said, "that *he* should be comforting *me*." The two became friends, and when Moreton suffered from appendicitis, Pyle and his wife invited her to recover from her illness in their apartment. Moreton stayed there for three or four weeks and recalled waking up in the mornings to the sound of Jerry playing the piano. When Pyle left for the office, Jerry would look up words in the dictionary and read books.

Moreton also recalled that people were always dropping by to visit the Pyles. Although often tired from his work, Pyle never refused a visitor. Drinks were served and a visitor might ask Jerry to read some poetry. "We would sit around, some on the floor, all at her feet the moment she began to read," said Moreton. "It was an enthralling experience."

In 1930 Miller left his job as managing editor of the *Daily News* for work with other newspapers in the Scripps-Howard chain. Miller's replacement at the newspaper, however, did not work out, and in 1932 Lowell Mellet, the newspaper's editor-in-chief, offered Miller's old job to Pyle. Although taking such a post meant giving up the independence he loved as a columnist, Pyle, after consulting Jerry, accepted the position. Those involved in aviation were heartsick about losing Pyle. To show their affection for his efforts on their behalf, a group of pilots had Earhart present Pyle with a watch at a special ceremony at the Washington-Hoover Airport. Pyle wore the watch for the rest of his life.

For the next three years, Pyle oversaw the newspaper's daily operation. He dealt with reporters and planned what stories went into each day's edition. The job proved to be "hard and fatiguing work," said Pyle, who missed being able to write on a daily basis. He did become a good manager, always working to support his staff. The 1930s were a hard time for businesses, including newspapers, as the Great Depression tightened its grip on the nation's economy. When management at the *Daily News* cut the pay of young copy boys from $10 a week to $9 a week, the crafty Pyle made up the difference by giving them a $1 expense voucher each week.

Although Pyle grew weary of the day-to-day grind of his job, he nevertheless tried to faithfully fulfill his duties. In memos sent to his staff, he

Friends and family often went with Pyle as he gathered information for the *Daily News*. During a visit to a Washington airport, he is joined by his wife, Jerry (second from left), and his good friend, Paige Cavanaugh (far right).

outlined his ideas about writing. He encouraged reporters to have people want to read the paper "by making it so alert and saucy and important that they will be afraid of missing something if they don't read it." In addition, he outlined tips for reporting stories that closely followed the style he would use in his future articles. "Write a story as tho[ugh] it were a privilege for you to write it," he advised. "Put some sauciness and sparkle into it. You don't have to be smart-alecky or pseudo-funny. Be human. Try to write like people talk."

In December 1934 Pyle suffered another in a long line of illnesses. His doctor advised him to take a trip to a warm climate. Pyle and Jerry climbed into their Ford automobile and set out for warmer temperatures. Unfortunately for Pyle, cold, wet weather followed him as he traveled to such states as Alabama, Mississippi, Arizona, New Mexico, and California. Despite the bad weather, Pyle and his wife developed a fondness for New Mexico, becoming close friends with Edward Shaffer, editor of the *Albuquerque Tribune*.

In Los Angeles, California, the Pyles booked passage on a freighter, the *Harpoon*, for a three-week voyage through the Panama Canal to Philadelphia, Pennsylvania. The slow journey aboard ship did wonders for Pyle's health. "I wish it had taken three years," Pyle later said of the voyage. He enjoyed spending time with a new friend, Walter A. Folger of Oregon, an older man who had traveled the world. "After knowing him for a little while," Pyle said of Folger, "I came very close to wishing sincerely that I were already old. It all seemed too simple; all the trouble behind, nothing important ahead, and the present quite good enough."

When Pyle returned to work at the *Daily News*, one of the newspaper's top syndicated columnists, Heywood Broun, was on vacation. To fill the space, Pyle received approval from his bosses to write a series of articles—eleven in all—about his trip. The articles were a hit with the newspaper's readers.

Years earlier, Pyle had said in a conversation with fellow Hoosier Abe Martin that his "idea of a good newspaper job would be just to travel around wherever you'd want to without any assignment except to write a story every day about what you'd seen." Encouraged by the success of his travel articles, Pyle came up with the idea of leaving his job as managing editor and becoming a roving columnist for Scripps-Howard.

Although well liked by his staff at the *Daily News*, Pyle never enjoyed his time as the newspaper's managing editor.

The idea drew the interest of Scripps-Howard editors, including George B. "Deac" Parker. According to Parker, Pyle's vacation articles possessed "a sort of Mark Twain quality and they knocked my eyes right out." Parker approved Pyle's idea of writing a column to be published six days a week with Lee Miller serving as his editor, or "vice president in charge of Pyle," as Miller said.

Pyle's column would appear regularly in the *Daily News* and also be distributed to the twenty-four newspapers in the Scripps-Howard chain. "I will go where I please and write what I please," Pyle said in a letter to a friend. "It's just the kind of job I've always wanted and I hope I make a go of it." The reporter had embarked on a journey that would last almost seven years and take him to each of the then forty-eight states and beyond.

On his journeys around the United States and to foreign countries as a roving columnist, Pyle packed light. He usually traveled with only one suit and one pair of pants.

Chapter 4

On the Road

★

Clem "Pop" Shaffer, the owner of the only hotel in Mountainair, New Mexico, was sitting in front of a fireplace in the lobby of his brick establishment in May 1942 when he noticed a slight, thin man walk into the room. The man, Ernie Pyle, joined him near the warmth of the fire and said he was looking for someone named Pop Shaffer. "You don't have to go any farther," said Shaffer, as the two men shook hands. Pyle had come to talk with Shaffer about his hobby of carving animal figures from wooden branches and roots.

As the two men talked, they discovered they both were from Indiana. After a tour of the hotel and lunch (a meal Pyle described as "the best food I have eaten since my mother's"), Shaffer took the reporter to his ranch and showed him his collection of carved wooden animals. While there, Pyle asked Shaffer "so many questions" he could not remember all of them.

The interview ended back at the hotel, where Pyle inspected the first two silver dollars Shaffer had made when he opened his hotel in 1924. He then sat down with Shaffer to talk some more before leaving late that afternoon to write two columns based on his day with the hotel owner and artist.

Shaffer is just one of the thousands of unique individuals Pyle tracked down to talk with during his days as a roving columnist for the Scripps-Howard chain of newspapers from 1935 to early 1942. His job, as Pyle saw it, involved "just writing about anything interesting I bump into." He proudly claimed that during his travels nobody ever turned down his request to talk to them. "Only one man has ever refused to let me write about him," he wrote, "and even he was friendly and we talked for an hour."

Published under the title "Hoosier Vagabond," Pyle's column became popular with readers looking for relief from such matters as the country's economic struggle during the Great Depression and the possibility of war in Europe with the rise of dictators such as Adolf Hitler in Germany and Benito Mussolini in Italy. Readers longing to break free from their boring lives were thrilled to read about Pyle's descriptions of exotic locations. They wished they could be with him on mornings when he and Jerry would pack their car, check out of their hotel, fill the car with gas, and "light out into open country."

Pyle also used himself as a character in his column, writing about his early life growing up in Dana, Indiana. Readers came to know much about his father, mother, and Aunt Mary. They laughed when reading about Pyle's misadventures with a stuck zipper on his pants and expressed concern about his health when he complained about his frequent bouts with colds. Those who read Pyle regularly, noted his friend Lee Miller, who edited his work, came to see the column as a "sort of cross between a travelogue, a highly personalized and humanized diary, and a reporting job."

When the nearly thirty-five-year-old Ernie Pyle set out from Washington, D.C., on August 2, 1935, with his wife to tour the country and report on what he found, traveling by automobile proved to be a difficult and long task. "I have no home," Pyle observed in one of his columns. "My home is where my extra luggage is, and where the car is stored, and where I happen to be getting mail this time. My home is America."

During the late 1930s and early 1940s, there existed no smooth system of interstate highways linking together American cities. Instead of connecting to the Internet, typing in a street address, and receiving accurate directions to a location, travelers had to rely on often undependable maps.

43

Hotels became a home-away-from-home for Pyle as he tracked down stories for his column. Joining her husband on his trips, Jerry worked on crossword puzzles and worked on such hobbies as making handbags.

Also, there were no nationwide hotel chains offering clean and dependable accommodations for the night, nor fast-food franchises or restaurant chains dotting the landscape.

The Pyles, however, were well suited to life on the road. Neither cared much for dining on fine food, gathering material possessions, or owning the latest fashions. Their luggage consisted of six suitcases and satchels. The backseat of the couple's Ford coupe became filled with books and copies of the *New Yorker* magazine, which both loved to read. As Pyle drove to his next assignment, Jerry, whom he identified in his column as "That Girl who rides with me," worked on the crossword puzzles she enjoyed solving. "My arms never get tired, even on rough roads," wrote Pyle. "But being a skinny fellow, I do get to hurting where I sit down, and I think I'll have to get an air cushion to sit on."

Although when he first set out Pyle drove as fast as seventy miles an hour as he drove around the country, he later discovered that such a high

speed was too much for travel on a daily basis. From then on, he drove at approximately forty miles an hour. "After all, why should I hurry?" Pyle asked. "I ain't goin' no place especially, as they say. And I got all day to get there."

Usually Pyle traveled anywhere from twenty-five miles to as much as three hundred miles per day. In one year, he noted that he drove a total of twenty-seven thousand miles and had only one flat tire. He rarely, if ever, ran out of gas. Each time that happened, thieves had siphoned the fuel out of the car's gas tank.

Tracking down possible stories in every state and such faraway places as Alaska, Hawaii, Canada, South America, and Central America, Pyle traveled by automobile, train, airplane, boat, and horse. In his travels, Pyle wore out two cars, five sets of tires, and three typewriters.

Scripps-Howard paid for all his expenses, but Pyle did not live a luxurious life on the road, especially when it came to meals. Breakfast for the

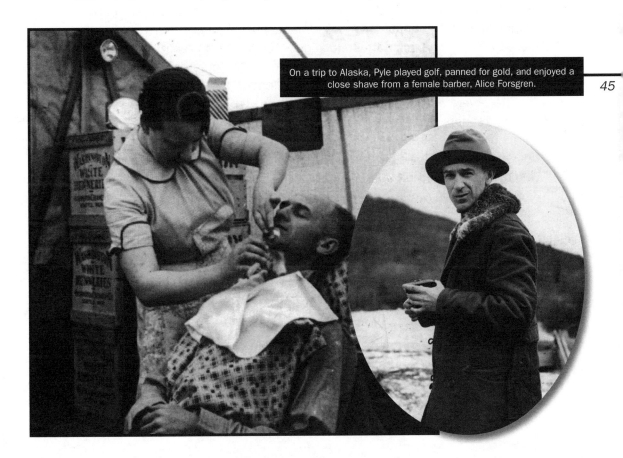

On a trip to Alaska, Pyle played golf, panned for gold, and enjoyed a close shave from a female barber, Alice Forsgren.

reporter usually included a glass of orange juice, a boiled egg, bacon, dry toast, and a cup of coffee or a glass of milk. Because he did not like to waste time eating lunch, Pyle would snack on a piece of fruit or a chocolate bar. He also told his readers that he could find an "excellent" dinner most places in the United States at a cost of anywhere from fifty to eighty-five cents.

Pyle hated to drive at night, so when dusk approached he and Jerry consulted a hotel directory published by the American Automobile Association for a suitable place to spend the night. Always concerned with keeping expenses to a minimum, Pyle usually selected a medium-priced hotel. "I have had good hotel rooms for 75 cents, and bad ones for $5," he said, estimating that no more than one out of twenty hotel rooms he and his wife stayed at had terrible conditions.

There were times when Pyle woke up in the middle of the night in a strange hotel room and forgot what city he was in. But in all his busy years of traveling, he left behind only one item—a toothbrush. The worst part of staying in a different hotel every night came from the lack of taste shown by the people who managed these lodgings. They failed to realize, Pyle noted, the importance to a traveler's happiness of such items as "a bed reading light, a floor lamp, an easy chair, fresh wallpaper, and clean curtains."

There were advantages, however, to a life filled with endless roving. Pyle told his readers that he never had to make his own bed, buy coal for heating a home, or wake up at four in the morning to milk the cows. He enjoyed hearing from the public via their letters and found there were even "fanatics who thrill me by vowing that there is a certain quality in my writings that on some days actually make sense."

When he came to a strange town, Pyle, hoping to learn about possible subjects to write about, would visit the local newspaper office and ask editors and reporters about interesting people who lived in the community. Other sources of information he sought out included a town's chief of police or a doctor. In addition, he took with him on his travels a small wooden box filled with index cards, organized by state and filled with story ideas sent to him by friends and fans.

Those featured in Pyle's columns seemed to be just ordinary people leading ordinary lives. The veteran reporter, however, always seemed able to uncover interesting tidbits to entertain and inform his readers. Harold Korb may have seemed like an ordinary salesman to his Evansville neighbors, but Pyle discovered that Korb had been named as the champion ice-cream soda maker for his Mellow-Cream Chocolate Soda at a convention of ice-cream salesmen from all over the country. Patrons of a Knoxville, Tennessee, restaurant probably never noticed the cook, William Andrew Johnson, but Pyle pointed out that Johnson happened to be the only living ex-slave of a president (Andrew Johnson).

Pyle's readers were also delighted by his visits to offbeat and exotic locations. Pyle drove over rutted roads to see a concrete marker indicating the spot where the corner of four states—Colorado, Utah, Arizona, and New Mexico—came together. He battled pesky mosquitoes and bitterly cold weather on a horseback ride through the Cascade Mountains in the state of Washington.

Although newspaper editors viewed Pyle's column as a way to entertain their readers, the Hoosier reporter explored serious subjects as well. He produced a series of columns on the extreme drought suffered by the Great Plains and Southwest states during the Great Depression.

Pyle called the area, which came to be known as the Dust Bowl, the "saddest land" he had ever seen in his life. Visiting western Kansas, Pyle observed nothing left. "There was not a tree, or a blade of grass, or a dog or a cow, or

LIBRARY OF CONGRESS

A farm near Dalhart, Texas, shows the destructive effects of the Dust Bowl in an image taken by famed photographer Dorothea Lange for the federal government's Farm Security Administration in the 1930s.

a human being—nothing whatever," he wrote. "The humans had given up, and gone. It was death, if I have ever seen death."

During a 1937 trip to the Hawaiian Islands, Pyle spent four days at the Kalaupapa leper colony, a place where those suffering from leprosy (a disfiguring illness today known as Hansen's disease) were cared for and kept apart from the rest of society. "Of all the places I've ever been," Pyle wrote Miller, "Kalaupapa to me is the most powerful and dramatic experience." He expressed pride at the work he did on the leper colony, noting it seemed to be the first newspaper report that "had not been distorted, over-dramatized and fictionalized." Readers agreed; a paper in Oklahoma reprinted the series and distributed two thousand copies to the public.

Pyle seldom took notes when he interviewed a subject for his column. Instead, he relied on his excellent memory. On one trip to Maine, he unearthed a half-dozen stories in less than two hours. Visiting the state of Washington, Pyle worked an entire week on one story. "Sometimes I can write a story in half an hour," he said. "Other times, when I am out of the mood, I start a story and never do get it finished." More often than not, however, he gathered material for a number of columns and then retreated to a hotel room to write for a few days, typing his stories on a portable Underwood typewriter.

Once he finished his work, Pyle sent his columns back to the *Daily News* office in Washington, D.C., by first-class mail. In all the years he traveled throughout America, the postal service never misplaced one of his columns. Because he moved from place to place, Pyle had little chance to see his published work. "Once I went for five months without seeing my own column in print," he said.

His friends and some of his readers may have believed Pyle had an easy job, but writing a column six days a week proved to be a demanding occupation. "They don't know what it is to drive and dig up information all day long, and then work till midnight writing it," he said. "One story a day sounds as easy as falling off a log. Try it sometime." Pyle said that his day consisted of five halves—one half gathering information, one half writing a column, one half seeing old friends in various cities, one half traveling, and one half sleeping.

The hard work done by Pyle paid off. Fellow reporters and Scripps-

Almost buried under the traditional leis given to him by friends as he sailed home to the United States, Pyle takes a last look at the Hawaiian Islands. During his time in Hawaii, he wrote several well regarded columns about a leper colony.

ERNIE PYLE STATE HISTORIC SITE

Howard editors praised his writing. One Cleveland columnist called Pyle the best reporter in the United States. Walter Morrow, editor of the *Rocky Mountain News* in Denver, Colorado, said Pyle's column was "without a doubt the most widely read thing in the paper." Polls conducted by newspapers in Evansville and Pittsburgh indicated that the roving reporter's work was popular with older readers as well as high school and college students. Lee Hills,

editor of the *Oklahoma News*, said his subscribers often commented, "Ernie Pyle does the things that we ourselves would like to do."

After a meeting of Scripps-Howard editors in June 1936, Frank Ford, editor of the *Evansville Press*, applauded Pyle's work in a letter to his parents in Dana, Indiana. At first, said Ford, his newspaper used only a few of Pyle's columns. "Then readers started calling up and writing in about them," Ford wrote, until the editors "were practically forced to use them daily, regardless of how badly the space was needed for other things." If the *Press* ever failed to publish even one of Pyle's reports, he continued, outraged subscribers would immediately call the newspaper to complain.

The daily grind of life on the road, however, took its toll on the roving reporter. Pyle often worried that there might come a point when his creativity

ERNIE PYLE STATE HISTORIC SITE

The Pyles arrive in Lima, Peru, from a stay in Ecuador during a trip to South America for Pyle's column.

49

might dry up and he would be unable to write his column. "I feel that my stuff at its very best is only just barely good enough," he wrote to Miller. When Pyle became depressed about his work, Jerry came to his rescue, praising what she liked and even helping type columns when needed.

Pyle took his writing very seriously and could be very protective about his columns. In a letter to Miller from a hotel in Denver, Pyle said that the last time he had seen a copy of his column he noted that the editor had deleted most of the "'little stuff' in my copy—the little personal phrases and opinions and asides, the stuff that I know . . . readers do like to see, maybe just a word here and there, but really the heart of the thing."

In the letter, Pyle also attempted to explain to Miller the process he used to write a column. When describing a particular scene or feeling, Pyle tried to make his words "sound almost like music, and I think sometimes it does, and I think it does to readers, even though they may not be specifically conscious of it." Dropping a word or cutting one sentence into two shorter ones, he added, "destroys the whole rhythm of it."

In March 1938 Pyle found himself in Hollywood, California, attempting to write a series of columns on movie stars. He also spent time considering the possibility of having his column offered for sale to newspapers outside of the Scripps-Howard chain. Although Pyle appreciated the chance to earn more money, he worried about losing his freedom. "The thing that frightens me worst is that if the thing should go over and get to running in a lot of papers," he wrote Miller, "then a fellow would feel like he couldn't quit if he wanted to. And that's always been part of my happiness in a job, that I felt the independence to quit a job anytime, even though I haven't exercised it but once or twice."

The Pyles, however, paid a price for their freedom. Both Pyle and his wife were heavy abusers of alcohol at times. In addition, Jerry developed an addiction to prescription drugs and suffered from depression. Pyle's friend Paige Cavanaugh observed of Jerry that it did not matter if she sat in a hotel room in Kansas City or Rio de Janeiro, as she never looked out of the window. Instead, she preferred to spend her time sitting in her room drinking, reading, and working on crossword puzzles.

(Right) The Pyle home in Albuquerque, New Mexico. (Opposite) Leaning in to offer Pyle advice on repairing a fence is Shirley Mount, the daughter of Earl Mount, one of the contractors who built the house. In the background is Dick Simmons, who did yard work for the Pyles.

ERNIE PYLE STATE HISTORIC SITE

In June 1940 Pyle bought land about three miles from downtown Albuquerque, New Mexico, on which to build a home. The couple had developed a deep fondness for the Southwest in particular and New Mexico specifically. Pyle wrote his parents in Dana that he and Jerry planned on living in New Mexico "with one idea: that we could come here and rest and be ourselves away from [all] the people."

Built by local contractors Earl Mount and Arthur McCollum, the home cost $3,848 and sat halfway between the local airport and a house belonging to good friends of the Pyles, Edward and Liz Shaffer. In a low moment, Pyle described the 1,145-square-foot house as a "regular little boxed-up mass production shack in a cheap new suburb." Later, he grew fond of his home, noting that its location offered a "terrific view" and "it's really as big as we will ever need."

As Pyle had been traveling around the United States reporting on quirky stories of American originals, Europe became engulfed in another war. Nazi Germany's invasion of Poland on September 1, 1939, had sparked declarations of war from the allied powers, Great Britain and France. After a period of quiet—a time that came to be known as the "phony war"—Germany had unleashed its powerful military machine, invading and taking control of Denmark, Holland, and Belgium. France finally surrendered on June 22, 1940.

German troops parade through Warsaw, Poland, in September 1939. The German invasion sparked a declaration of war from both Great Britain and France.

The bulk of British troops and some French forces had managed to make their way back to England, which now stood alone against Nazi Germany. In a speech before England's House of Commons, Prime Minister Winston Churchill, the leader of the British government, vowed to "defend our Island, whatever the cost may be, we shall fight on the beaches . . . we shall never surrender."

In preparation for a possible invasion of Great Britain, the German air force, the Luftwaffe, flew across the English Channel to drop bombs on English cities. Determined pilots from the Royal Air Force took to their Hurricane and Spitfire fighter aircraft to challenge the Luftwaffe's bombers—the Battle of Britain had begun.

The war raging in Europe divided public opinion in the United States. The stunning success of Hitler's Nazi Germany and its brutal treatment of Jews and others who opposed it helped to create much sympathy for England's plight. But there existed in the country a powerful group of isolationists who believed America should not involve itself in the foreign conflict. Famous flier Charles A. Lindbergh served as a key spokesman for the isolationist America First Committee, formed in 1940 to argue the case against U.S. involvement in the war.

Adolf Hitler (center), the leader of Nazi Germany, tours Paris, France, after his troops captured the city in June 1940.

Pyle felt the pull of war, as he had when his friend Thad Hooker had left Dana to join the army in 1918. There grew in the forty-year-old Pyle an "overpowering urge to be there amidst it all." The feeling he had did not come from a curiosity to travel or a journalistic need to report on a story, but because Pyle "simply wanted to go privately—just inside myself I wanted to go."

If he avoided the opportunity to see firsthand a nation at war and to share the experience with others, Pyle reasoned, it would mean he had become "disinterested in living." With his decision made, Pyle consulted with Scripps-Howard editors in Washington, D.C., about his plans. They agreed to send him to England.

The decision to travel to a country under attack, placing himself in harm's way, did not come easy for Pyle. "I am scared half to death," he admitted to a friend, "and Jerry is badly upset and really grieving." Despite her worries, Jerry was there to see Pyle off as he sailed from America on-

St. Paul's Cathedral in London can be seen through the smoke and haze caused by the great fire raid of December 29, 1940.

U.S. NATIONAL ARCHIVES

board the S.S. *Exeter* on November 16, 1940. The ship docked in Lisbon, Portugal, and after a few days of waiting Pyle took a flight to England, arriving on December 9.

The first words Pyle heard upon arriving by train in London were spoken by an old porter who helped him with his bags. "Well, he [the Luftwaffe] hasn't come yet, sir," the porter told Pyle, "he's more than a bit late tonight." There were no air raids on London the first few nights of Pyle's visit. From his room at the Savoy Hotel, for which he paid twenty-three shillings ($4.60) per day, he wrote Jerry that he had received courteous and kindly treatment from everyone. "And I fell in love with England the minute I set foot ashore," Pyle wrote.

Pyle did not have long to wait to feel the full effect of the German air assault on London. On Sunday, December 29, the Luftwaffe sent more than a hundred planes to drop incendiaries (bombs designed to cause fires) on the English capital. Working in his room at the Savoy Hotel, Pyle could feel the building shake as British anti-aircraft guns fired at the enemy planes. "You could hear the boom, crump, crump, crump of heavy bombs at their work of tearing buildings apart," he later wrote. "They were not too far away."

Instead of retreating to the hotel's sturdy bomb shelter, Pyle and a few of his friends went out on a high balcony that gave a good view of the London skyline. Fires had broken out all over the city. Some of the fires were near enough for Pyle to hear the flames crackle and firemen yell to one another. Writing Miller about his experience, Pyle said he felt like he was "a spectator at some huge show."

Looking out over London, Pyle said he would remember forever the sight of the great city "stabbed with great fires, shaken by explosions . . . all of it roofed over with a ceiling of pink that held bursting shells, balloons, flares, and the sound of vicious engines." He called what he saw "the most hateful, most beautiful single scene I have ever known."

In addition to reporting on the German bombing raids, Pyle visited a number of air-raid shelters, spent time with a crew manning an anti-aircraft gun, and talked to ordinary British citizens about their responses to the bombing. Pyle became "terribly impressed" with the British people through these face-to-face meetings. "I've never seen anything like it," he wrote Miller. "The people are determined to win this war, and if they don't it will be the leaders' fault, and not the people. Despite all this bombing, they don't feel they have been hurt at all, and consider their refusal to collapse as an absolute victory over Hitler's bombing of London, which in truth it was."

Pyle poses on a rooftop in London during his days reporting on the bombing of the city by the German air force. The pump and water were used to douse any incendiary bomb that might fall on the roof during an air raid.

Pyle's columns from London were an immediate hit with American readers. Miller told his friend that his "marvelous stuff" received "terrific play" in a number of American newspapers. Roy W. Howard, Scripps-Howard president, also sent a congratulatory note to Pyle on January 10, 1941. Howard applauded the columnist's work, calling it the "most illuminating human and appealing descriptive matter" ever printed in America since the start of the Battle of Britain. The warm congratulations from his boss gave Pyle such a bad case of stage fright, he wrote his wife, that he had hardly "been able to write a line since."

A few months into his assignment in England, however, Pyle received some bad news from back home. On March 3, 1941, his mother died after suffering a stroke. Pyle and a friend had left their hotel for dinner when a bellboy from the Savoy caught up with them and handed a telegram to Pyle informing him of his mother's death.

When he returned to his darkened room, Pyle remembered "little pictures" of his mother's life, including her attending neighborhood square dances, playing the violin, aiding sick animals, driving the family automobile in the local Fourth of July parade, and crying as he left to report for service with the naval reserve in World War I. "The pictures grew older," said Pyle. "Gradually she became stooped, and toil-worn, and finally white and wracked with age . . . but always spirited, always sharp."

Pyle returned to the United States in late March 1941, carrying with him in his luggage a dud German incendiary device and fragments from German bombs. After visiting with his father and Aunt Mary in Dana, he returned to his new home in Albuquerque hoping

ERNIE PYLE STATE HISTORIC SITE

After returning from London, Pyle works in the study of his Albuquerque home. The cartoon to Pyle's right was drawn by David Low, one of Britain's greatest cartoonists. A piece of a German bomb had damaged the drawing, and Low wrote on it: "Dear Hitler: Thanks for the criticism."

The battleship USS *Arizona* burns after being hit by Japanese bombs during the attack on the American naval base at Pearl Harbor, Hawaii, on December 7, 1941.

U.S. NATIONAL ARCHIVES

to relax and finish some final columns on his experiences in England. He had become so popular, however, that people from all over came to his home hoping to see him in the flesh. The racket grew so great that Pyle had to abandon his home and find a hotel room where he could write in peace.

The separation had not been easy on the Pyles' marriage. As Pyle continued to travel to unearth ideas for his column, Jerry's mental condition worsened. She even made an unsuccessful attempt to commit suicide. Her problem with alcohol had gotten so bad that she had nearly died from a bleeding stomach. "My old life is gone," Pyle wrote Miller. "But it is a hard thing to abandon forever a companionship that was as close as ours was for fifteen years." Although he briefly considered quitting his job as a roving reporter for a return to "a settled life of office hours and drudgery," Pyle abandoned the idea, saying such a job would drive him crazy within six months.

Pyle decided that drastic measures needed to be taken and received permission from Scripps-Howard executives to take a three-month leave of absence, with pay, to care for Jerry. The leave failed to bring about any change for the better. "Nothing can help her," Pyle wrote a friend about Jerry, "and she can't, or won't. Everything looks blue."

Upon returning to his work, Pyle outlined a possible trip to the Orient to begin in December 1941, with stops in the Philippines, Hong Kong, Burma, China, and possibly Australia and New Zealand. Pyle's journey, however, took a backseat to the developing tension in the Pacific between the United States and Japan. He had to give up a seat on a flight to Hawaii to make room for the transport of war materials to American forces there.

The tensions between the two countries flamed into war on December 7, 1941, when Japanese planes attacked the American naval base at Pearl Harbor in Hawaii. The sneak attack achieved total surprise; nineteen U.S. ships from the Pacific fleet were either sunk or damaged, more than 250 planes were destroyed while still on the ground, and approximately 3,500 soldiers and sailors were killed or wounded.

On December 8, Congress approved President Franklin D. Roosevelt's call for a declaration of war against Japan. Three days later, Germany and Italy declared war on the United States. America had entered World War II.

President Franklin D. Roosevelt signs the declaration of war against Japan on December 8, 1941. The black armband Roosevelt wears on his left arm is in remembrance of his mother, who had died a few months before.

U.S. NATIONAL ARCHIVES

Americans were quick to rally around the war effort. In Terre Haute, Indiana, men register for the draft; citizens donate scrap aluminum; and a grocer checks a customer's ration book.

Chapter 5

At the Front

★

During the early 1940s, millions of American men waited anxiously for a notice from the federal government's Selective Service System. Sooner or later, factory workers, college students, and farmers received from their mailman a card with a notice beginning: "Greetings." Recipients of such a card had to report for induction into the armed forces. They were in the army now.

Those who became soldiers in the U.S. Army in World War II left civilian life for a potentially hazardous one facing German and Italian troops in Europe or Japanese forces in the Pacific. Their loved ones back home—fathers, mothers, sisters, brothers, and wives—were busy doing all they could to help the war effort. They planted Victory Gardens, collected scrap metal, and endured the rationing of such everyday items as meat, sugar, gasoline, and rubber. Anxious to know how the young American soldiers were dealing with their new lives, they turned to a trusted source: Ernie Pyle.

As he had during his days as a roving reporter, Pyle used his easy nature and modesty to get close to U.S. soldiers and to tell the story of their lives with the military to the regular readers of his column, featured in newspapers owned by Scripps-Howard and others throughout the country by way of the United Feature Syndicate. "I'm doing the same kind of stuff I've always done in the column," he told a reporter, "except that it's on a war basis. Instead of talking to civilians about civilian things, I just swapped over to the military."

The columns Pyle wrote about soldiers' lives away from home were popular with families in the United States. One soldier received a letter from his wife praising Pyle's work. "Wives and mothers who read him," the letter said, "must feel as grateful as I do to know certain things definitely—not just to be wondering about them." Best-selling books formed from Pyle's columns, *Here Is Your War* and *Brave Men*, helped add to his fame.

Through his work, Pyle also became the G.I.'s favorite war correspondent. Soldiers read his writing in clippings from local papers sent

No 466152 EA

UNITED STATES OF AMERICA
OFFICE OF PRICE ADMINISTRATION

4

WAR RATION BOOK FOUR

Issued to _Luella Runck_
(Print first, middle, and last name)

Complete address _Oxford, Indiana_

READ BEFORE SIGNING

In accepting this book, I recognize that it remains the property of the United States Government. I will use it only in the manner and for the purposes authorized by the Office of Price Administration.

Luella Runck
(Signature)

Void if Altered

It is a criminal offense to violate rationing regulations.

OPA Form R-145

A war ration book issued to Luella Runck of Oxford, Indiana, by the federal government's Office of Price Administration. Individuals used these books daily to purchase rationed goods such as sugar, butter, meat, and gasoline.

to them by their families and in the pages of *Stars and Stripes*, the army's daily newspaper. A visit to a unit by Pyle seemed to energize American troops. "My men always fought better when Ernie was around," General Omar Bradley told Pyle's Aunt Mary.

Pyle achieved his fame by getting close to the average soldier in World War II during a time of great personal crisis. On April 14, 1942, he and his wife, Jerry, were divorced. "It seemed to be a necessary and last-hope form of psychological surgery," Pyle wrote his friend and Scripps-Howard editor Lee Miller. "We are both terribly broken over it." Such a drastic action, Pyle hoped, might shock Jerry out of her depression and get her to alter her dependence on alcohol and drugs.

For a time, Jerry checked into a hospital before returning to Albuquerque, New Mexico, where she found a job as a clerk at Kirtland Field, an army airport in Albuquerque. Pyle kept hoping he and Jerry could be together again and continued to write her letters while he served as a war correspondent overseas. He even made the necessary legal arrangements so that the two could remarry without his presence.

In June 1942 Pyle left the United States and traveled to Great Britain to report on the American soldiers preparing for what they hoped might be the invasion of Europe and the defeat of Nazi Germany.

Pyle had an easy time talking with American troops. Many already knew his name from reading his column. He also decided not to wear an officer's uniform, which he was entitled to as a war correspondent. Wearing such a uniform would "scare them and put them on their guard, and I couldn't lie around half the night shooting the bull with them," said Pyle. He added that the soldiers treated him as "just another old broken-down guy from home and sort of a sight for sore eyes."

It was more than his civilian clothing and age that made soldiers trust Pyle. From the first, U.S. forces could see that the reporter had no problems in sharing their hardships. In one column about enlisted men training to become officers, Pyle joked that he had tried to participate in an obstacle course with the men, but instead of climbing a high wall he had stopped at the bottom and lit a cigarette. Actually, he had participated in the rugged course, earning the soldiers' respect in the process.

During his overseas assignment, Pyle thought he might revive his old aviation column by concentrating his reporting on the air corps, becoming that service's "unofficial biographer." He found his true subject, however, in North Africa, the scene of the United States's first large-scale combat operations in the European theater of war. There he began his love affair with the infantry, and the soldiers with him.

Military leaders for Great Britain and the United States were under great pressure to do something to strike back at Nazi Germany. Joseph Stalin, the leader of the Soviet Union's Communist government, had called for the opening of a "second front" to help his forces, who had been battling the Germans on the Russian front since June 1941.

American and English generals, however, disagreed on what would be the best way to hit the German army, the Wehrmacht. American generals, including Dwight D. Eisenhower, the commander of U.S. forces, argued that the fastest way to defeat the Nazis would be to land troops in France and drive straight on to the German capital, Berlin. British generals and their prime minister, Winston Churchill, were very reluctant to support such an effort by the untried American forces.

Instead of a cross-channel invasion of France from bases in England, the British called for landings in North Africa to seize control of the French colonies of Morocco, Algeria, and Tunisia. These colonies were under the rule of the French Vichy government, which had allied itself with Nazi Germany. Planners for the invasion hoped French troops would join the allied cause. The landings could also serve to support the British Eighth Army in Egypt and its struggle against German General Erwin Rommel's Afrika Korps and Italian forces, and give American soldiers a taste of what war was like.

After writing about American troops training in Ireland and England, Pyle joined a convoy for the invasion of North Africa. The "C" armband Pyle wears indicates his status as a war correspondent.

LILLY LIBRARY, INDIANA UNIVERSITY

Code-named Operation Torch, the landing of American soldiers in French Morocco, and Oran and Algiers in Algeria, occurred in early November 1942 and met with some success. After traveling on a convoy from England with U.S. soldiers, Pyle reached Oran on November 23, 1942. He stepped off the British transport ship *Rangitiki* dressed in an army uniform with an armband bearing the letter "C" for correspondent. He carried with him a bedroll, small knapsack, duffel bag, gas mask, helmet, canteen, and typewriter.

In his early columns from North Africa, Pyle reported on his experiences on the convoy and the stories of troops who had made the initial landings. Although he believed these pieces were "confusing and inadequate," Miller said they were "exciting" reading to those back in the United States. Pyle produced even more powerful reading with columns blasting the American policy of leaving in power French government officials who were sympathetic to the Nazi cause.

A number of correspondents in North Africa had attempted to report on the controversy, but their articles were stopped by army censors (all stories issued from combat areas had to be reviewed by censors overseas and in the United States). Pyle had learned about the trouble with the French officials from friends he had in the army's Counter Intelligence Corps. "We have left in office most of the small-fry officials put there by the Germans before we came," Pyle wrote in one column. "The loyal French see this and wonder what manner of people we are. Our enemies saw it, laughed, and called us soft."

Pyle managed to slip his reports by the censors through a bit of luck and chance. There had not been much for the censors to do in Oran, as most of the correspondents had left the area, so Pyle had established good relations with them. "The censors are so bored that when I bring my column in the entire office staff grabs for it and reads it hungrily," he noted, "everybody makes flattering remarks, and then we all go out and have a bite to eat." Probably, a censor saw Pyle's name with the articles, believed they contained their usual harmless material about soldiers' lives, and passed them to be published without actually reading the columns.

ERNIE PYLE STATE HISTORIC SITE

Pyle talks on a field telephone while reporting on the infantry in the hills of Tunisia. His stories of the struggles of the average soldier made Pyle famous back in the United States.

In early January 1943 Pyle traveled to an air base at Biskra in the Algerian desert and spent weeks there talking to fighter pilots and bomber crews about their missions against the Germans. Later that month, he visited the infantry, spending time with officers and enlisted men—privates, corporals, and sergeants. Unlike other correspondents, who had to write dispatches on the "big picture," the day-by-day movement of the war, Pyle could wander where he liked and write about whatever interested him.

The army placed few restrictions on Pyle. He could talk to whomever he wanted—infantrymen, artillerymen, tank crews, combat engineers, medics, doctors, and nurses. Traveling in an army jeep, sometimes alone and sometimes with another correspondent, Pyle would visit a particular unit, live with the men, share their struggles, and talk to them about their experiences in and out of combat.

Pyle soon became used to going for weeks without a bath, shaving and washing his feet about once a week in his steel helmet, and sleeping on the ground without proper cover for the cold desert nights. He wrote his friend Paige Cavanaugh that life on the front became very simple. Pyle said there were only four essential items—clothes, food, cigarettes, and "whatever portion of safety you can manage to arrange for yourself."

Used to being on the road from his days as a roving reporter, Pyle adapted very well to life at the front lines. Jack Thompson, a war correspondent for the *Chicago Tribune*, remembered seeing Pyle at a new frontline headquarters in Tunisia preparing a spot on which to sleep during the night.

Pyle set out his bedroll under an abandoned farm wagon, cushioning the hard ground with straw. He found some strips of corrugated tin roofing and set them around three sides of the wagon, making walls. "Then with all his clothes on he crawled into his sack, pulled his old cap down tightly around his head, snuggled down and grinned," said Thompson. Pyle called his space "the coziest place I'd slept in for a week."

Writing Jerry in February 1943 about his experiences, Pyle noted that time seemed to stand still when he visited the front. "Time has no meaning; you never know what day it is," he said, "sometimes you can't even guess the date within a week."

There were other changes in Pyle as well. Driving in an open jeep in the cold weather gave the correspondent "a wind-burn tan like I've never had before in my life." He also noticed that he seemed to be hungry all the time, had even managed to gain some weight, and "truly have never felt better physically in my life."

According to Horace Miner, an officer who met Pyle in North Africa, the reporter never seemed to be trying "to get a story." Instead, he would rather spend his time talking about "old times, friends, and recent events." If he gained enough information for a column from these talks, Pyle would write one.

Three American soldiers from a tank destroyer unit take cover during a German bombing attack in the El Guettar Valley in Tunisia. The three men are (from left to right) Privates Thurman Reltor, Leon Jeannotte, and Chelsea Bate.

When he talked with soldiers, Pyle made sure to get their names and hometowns, writing them down in a small notebook he carried with him. He preferred not to take notes of his conversations because "a notebook and a fellow with a long pencil scare [the] hell out of a soldier, or anybody else."

After visiting with the troops, Pyle would return to army headquarters, located away from the fighting, for three or four days, writing a number of columns to send to Scripps-Howard. As he wrote, Pyle attempted to mentally carry himself "back to the time and place of the incident" he was writing about. Writing came hard to him, he admitted to another reporter, but once he had a column started he usually had no trouble in getting it finished.

Don Whitehead, a reporter who covered the war for United Press, which supplied articles to newspapers across the United States, observed that Pyle would write approximately fifteen hundred words and then spend several hours "carefully editing, striking out paragraphs, re-wording phrases." Once Pyle had finished, the resulting column offered readers the work of a "great craftsman with an intense feeling for people," said Whitehead.

As he had when he reported on average people with interesting stories to tell during his days as a roving reporter, Pyle concentrated on giving his World War II audience a feel for the daily chores of life at the front. He talked about how soldiers would dig a small hole in the ground, pour gasoline into

Members of the First Armored Division presented Pyle with a captured German vehicle for "sweating it out with us at Faïd Pass."

the hole, light it, and then have a small fire on which they could heat up a cup of coffee. They turned five-gallon gasoline cans into cooking pots. To clean their mess kits without wasting water, a precious resource in desert warfare, the G.I.s scoured them with sand and polished them with toilet paper—"the best dishrag I've ever found," said Pyle.

There were some subjects, however, the army refused to allow correspondents to cover. While in North Africa, Pyle prepared a column on soldiers suffering from battle fatigue, also known as shell shock. These men could no longer take the stress of being in combat. Army censors stopped Pyle's work from appearing in the United States.

Pyle received a number of letters from readers praising his work. In a February 27, 1943, letter to Miller, Pyle said that the fan mail included remarks from readers saying the "small and descriptive stuff" he used in his column "is just what the people want to read." He also told Miller he had not yet had any close calls when near the scene of the fighting. "I try not to take any foolish chances," Pyle said, "but there's just no way to play it completely safe and still do your job. The front does get into your blood, and you miss it and want to go back."

In addition to receiving reports about how readers were enjoying his writing, Pyle received good news of a more personal nature on March 12, 1943. The London office of United Press sent him a telegram that it had heard from editors in New York he had remarried his former wife.

A delighted Pyle cabled Jerry the following: "Just received word marriage from London. So happy could bust. Love you." Jerry told him that she and their dog, Cheetah, had settled into their Albuquerque home and were waiting for his safe return.

Pyle's identification with the infantry—the "mud-rain-frost-and-wind boys . . . that wars can't be won without"—became complete in April 1943 when he attached himself to the army's First Division as it moved against German forces holding the harbor at Bizerte in Tunisia. "Just returned last night from our little correspondents' camp after an incredible week right in the lines," Pyle wrote Miller on May 2. "This is a totally different type of warfare up here, and if you go and live with the troops . . . you're right in the thick of it. Was under constant fire for three days and nights, and it aint play."

By the middle of May, the battle for Tunisia had been won. American soldiers had become combat veterans and had paid a high price. At that time, army censors would halt any dispatches discussing the brutal realities of war—shrapnel from shells slicing off a soldier's arm or leg, or a direct hit from the dreaded German 88mm gun on an American Sherman tank, causing it to burst into flames and burning alive those trapped inside. The tank's armor could not muffle the screams of its crew.

Pyle did manage to make readers of his column aware of the dramatic change that had come over U.S. troops as they experienced the horrors of combat. Once he had sat down to rest at the front with the First Division when a platoon of tired soldiers passed by. "Their faces are black and unshaven," Pyle wrote. "They are young men, but the grime and whiskers and exhaustion make them look middle-aged. They are just guys from Brooklyn and Main Street, but you wouldn't remember them. They are too far away now. They are too tired."

At the completion of the North Africa campaign, Pyle found himself popular with both the troops in the field and the reading public back home. Don Coe, a United Press reporter who had traveled with Pyle in North Africa, noted that the first question asked him by every soldier was if he knew Ernie Pyle. A grateful member of the First Armored Division presented the reporter with a captured German Volkswagen staff car. Pyle eventually had to turn the car over to American military officials, but said he preferred the American jeep anyway.

Readership of Pyle's column also soared. In November 1942 Pyle's work had been distributed by Scripps-Howard and United Feature in 42 newspapers. By April 1943 that number had grown to 122 newspapers with a total circulation of nine million readers.

On June 29, 1943, Pyle traveled by plane for Bizerte, where he boarded the USS *Biscayne*, flagship for the upcoming invasion of the Italian island of Sicily in the

ERNIE PYLE STATE HISTORIC SITE

Secure in his Mae West life jacket, Pyle prepares for the invasion of Sicily onboard the USS *Biscayne*.

American General George S. Patton displays some German bullets to Pyle and Chris Cunningham, a United Press reporter, during the fighting in Sicily.

Mediterranean Sea. Code-named Operation Husky, the campaign against the approximately 300,000 Italian and German troops on the island lasted only five weeks. Once Allied forces had secured the island, they planned to press on to invade Italy and knock that country out of the war.

During his time on the *Biscayne*, Pyle gathered material for columns on the navy and also wrote and edited the ship's daily newspaper. He also witnessed the *Biscayne*'s young crew's first taste of battle with German planes while still in the harbor in Bizerte. Three men were wounded in the attack, but gun crews shot down the enemy aircraft.

By the time the Sicily invasion was well in hand, the hard fighting had begun to have an effect on Pyle. "I'm getting awfully tired of war and writing about it," he wrote his wife. "It seems like I can't think of anything new to say—each time it's like going to the same movie again."

When a fellow correspondent returned to Washington, D.C., and told Miller that Pyle had begun to look worn out, the editor sent his friend a telegram urging him home for a vacation. Even before receiving Miller's message, Pyle had decided he needed a rest. "Have just sort [of] bogged down and feel [I] need mental refreshing," he informed Miller.

Pyle returned to Algeria and flew on to Morocco to catch a plane for the trip back to the United States. He arrived at LaGuardia Field in New York very early in the morning on September 7, 1943. Four days before, British troops had made the initial landings on the mainland of Italy. As Allied forces continued to pound away at the enemy, an exhausted Pyle prepared to get a little rest. It turned out that he had little opportunity to do so.

Once Pyle checked into his room at the Algonquin Hotel in New York City, he and Miller talked while watching "the Empire State building materialize out of the fog," Miller remembered. At about eight in the morning, the two men decided to get some rest. "And within ten minutes," said Miller, "the ring of the phone shattered our dazed sleep."

Reporters wanted to interview Pyle for their newspapers, photographers clamored to take his picture, army intelligence officers wanted to question him about his experiences with the troops, radio people wanted him to make broadcasts, and wives and friends of soldiers wanted to know about their loved ones overseas. There were so many demands on his time that he almost went crazy, Pyle wrote his father. One of the few requests Pyle accepted was to appear with Henry Morgenthau, U.S. secretary of the treasury, on the radio program *We the People* to promote the sale of bonds to help the war effort.

The crush of well-wishers continued when Pyle journeyed to Washington, D.C., to meet with Scripps-Howard officials. While there, he also learned that Lester Cowan, a Hollywood producer, wanted to make a movie based on his columns about the infantry—a film that became *The Story of G.I. Joe.* Miller tried, and failed, to pro-

Returning to the United States as a celebrity thanks to his reporting from North Africa, Pyle received numerous requests for interviews and radio programs. Here, he is interviewed by Henry Morgenthau Jr., the secretary of the treasury, in a program broadcast from Monticello, the home of Thomas Jefferson.

ERNIE PYLE STATE HISTORIC SITE

tect his friend from the crush of attention. "The merry-go-round was running at full speed and he couldn't get off," Miller said of Pyle.

Pyle tried not to let his fame go to his head. He noted in one column that there were advantages to all the attention. Store clerks would offer him hard-to-find items, railroad and airline clerks could find seats for him when others had been turned away, and plumbers and typewriter repairmen came when he called. "I think that on the whole I'm fairly safe from the perils of celebrity," Pyle said. "For one thing it came too late. I'm forty-three, and it doesn't matter so much any more."

On his return home to Albuquerque, Pyle did have some time to relax with Jerry and Cheetah and to meet with his old friend from Indiana University, Paige Cavanaugh. Still, he had to deal with bushels of fan mail from all over the country and a constantly ring-

ERNIE PYLE STATE HISTORIC SITE

Home from the war, Pyle relaxes with his father, Will, in front of a store in downtown Dana, Indiana.

ing telephone. The turmoil surrounding his visit proved to be too much for Jerry, who suffered a breakdown and had to be hospitalized for a few days. "I can hardly look at her," Pyle told a friend, "without kind of crying inside at her awful tragedy—and mine."

Jerry's breakdown might also have been caused by Pyle's decision to return to cover the fighting in Italy, equipped this time with a wool-lined sleeping bag given to him by his wife as a going-away present. Pyle did not look forward to going back to the front. "But what can a guy do?" he asked. "There are millions of others who are reluctant too, and they can't even get home." In late November 1943 he left the United States for the war and further fame.

Pyle visits with nurses from the Fifty-sixth Evacuation Hospital during a visit to the Anzio battlefield on March 18, 1944.

Chapter 6

Captain Waskow

★

In December 1943 Ernie Pyle returned from several days at the front in Italy. He had been with the Thirty-sixth Infantry Division as it battled German troops on the way to capture Rome, the Italian capital. While with the American G.I.s, he had gathered material on the fighting on Mount Sammucro, also called Hill 2105. The action had been intense. The mountain's slopes had been so steep that soldiers had to use mules to carry supplies up the hill and dead and wounded men back down.

Now safe at the headquarters of General Mark Clark's Fifth Army at Caserta, located north of Naples, Pyle shared a room with two other correspondents, Reynolds Packard of the United Press and Clark Lee of the International News Service. There Pyle tried to write about the tough fighting being waged on the Italian front.

The Mediterranean country's hilly terrain, mixed with the cold, wet winter weather, had made conditions very difficult for American soldiers. "The country was shockingly beautiful," Pyle told his readers, "and just as shockingly hard to capture from the enemy." The Germans held on stubbornly to their positions and American troops gained only a yard or foot at a time. The opposing armies were so close together that they sometimes threw rocks at each other.

The bloodshed he had witnessed, in addition to the frigid temperatures he had endured, had depressed Pyle. He wrote his wife Jerry that he had seen "too many dead men, and wounded and exhausted ones, for the good of the soul."

Pyle's bad mood may have contributed to a crisis in confidence about his writing. Don Whitehead, an Associated Press reporter who had known Pyle since North Africa, remembered coming back from the front one evening to find his friend worried about three columns he had recently finished,

Captain Henry T. Waskow of Belton, Texas, and the front page of the *Washington Daily News* that featured Pyle's column on Waskow's death.

ERNIE PYLE STATE HISTORIC SITE

but not yet sent to his editor, Lee Miller. "I've lost the touch," Whitehead quoted Pyle as saying. "This stuff stinks. I feel stale and just can't seem to get going again."

Pyle tossed Whitehead the columns and asked him to read them and offer his opinion. The first column Whitehead picked up involved the death of a Captain Henry T. Waskow of Belton, Texas. Waskow had served as commander of Company B of the 143rd Infantry Regiment, Thirty-sixth Infantry Division. He had been killed near San Pietro on December 14, 1943, while battling against German forces in the mountains outside of Rome.

The men under his command had nothing but praise for the officer who led them into combat. His troops considered Waskow a fair man, and some looked up to him as though he were their father. "He always looked after us," said one of his men. "He'd go to bat for us every time." His concern for his men might have cost Waskow his life. Hearing the approach of an incoming German shell, the captain had pushed his messenger, Private Riley Tidwell, to the ground. Fragments from the shell hit Waskow in the chest, killing him.

Pyle stood at the foot of the mule trail when Waskow's body came down from the mountain. "Dead men had been coming down the mountain all evening, lashed onto the backs of mules," he said. As Waskow's body lay in the road alongside four other soldiers who had been killed, his men began to move closer to his body. "Not so much to look, I think," said Pyle, "as to say something in finality to him and to themselves."

As Pyle watched, he could see and hear the various reactions of the men as they paid their respects. Some of the soldiers were so upset all they could do was curse. Others spoke directly to Waskow and said how sorry they were about his death. Another G.I. held the officer's hand for five minutes without saying a word. Finally, the soldier "reached over and gently straightened the points of the captain's shirt collar, and then he sort of rearranged the tattered edges of the uniform around the wound," Pyle wrote, "and then he got up and walked away down the road in the moonlight, all alone."

Whitehead had tears in his eyes when he finished reading the column. "If this is a sample from a guy who has lost his touch," he said to Pyle, "then the rest of us had better go home." He showed the column to other war correspondents who agreed it stood as one of the finest Pyle had ever done. "This was the kind of writing all of us were striving for," Whitehead noted, "the picture we were trying to paint in words for the people at home."

Pyle's column, "The Death of Captain Waskow," did not appear in the United States until January 10, 1944, after the soldier's family had been notified of his death. The reporter's sincere description of the effect that the loss of a comrade had on a group of G.I.s touched readers everywhere. The soldier responsible for reading Pyle's column over short-wave radio from Italy to the United States so it could be published was so moved that he had to fight back tears as he read the words into the microphone.

Miller wrote Pyle on January 14 that the Waskow column had "knocked everybody for a loop." The *Washington Daily News* devoted its entire front page to the story, printing it five columns wide with no headline. The issue nearly sold out, with only thirty-nine copies returned to the paper from newsstands. Most of the Scripps-Howard newspapers had printed the column on their front pages, and a number of other papers across the country had also given the article page-one treatment. "In short," Miller told Pyle, "nice going, bub."

With his Waskow column, Pyle had reached the height of his career. His work appeared in approximately two hundred newspapers with a total circulation of thirteen million readers every day. While overseas, Pyle received a hundred fan letters a week from soldiers and readers in the United States. The popular picture magazine *Life* claimed that Pyle occupied a place in journalism "no other correspondent in this war has achieved."

Despite all the praise coming his way, however, Pyle felt down in the dumps. He attempted to wipe from his mind the memory of dead and dying men by drowning his sorrows over the Christmas season with liquor. "We're all so damned homesick and weary of the war," Pyle wrote Miller, "that it seems like a disease, and you take to the bottle now and then without planning on it."

No matter how much alcohol he drank, however, Pyle never lost his touch for the common man. After finishing work one night while at Caserta, Pyle and Whitehead went down to the officers' bar and had a few drinks. Pyle tried to start a conversation with a colonel standing beside the two men.

He received a rude response from the officer, who failed to recognize the famous correspondent because of his casual clothes. "You know," Pyle told the colonel, "I was going to buy you a drink because I thought you were nice people. But you aren't and I don't like to drink with people like you." Instead, Pyle and Whitehead went to a table where two second lieutenants were sitting with two nurses. They sat with them and spent the next several hours "talking about war, home, love, mud, the wounded," Whitehead remembered.

While in Italy, Pyle made frequent visits to the Anzio beachhead to report on the fighting there. He inspects a 155mm gun with (above, left) Corporal Jesse Cooper of Powell Station, Tennessee, and Private William Bennett of Dunn, North Carolina; escorts Second Lieutenant Berry Verazin of Nanticoke, Pennsylvania, a nurse with the Fifty-sixth Evacuation Hospital; and eats canned rations heated over a Coleman stove with members of a tank crew.

Although unhappy, Pyle did all he could to make life better for his fellow war correspondents. He visited them in the hospital when they fell sick or were wounded and shared his food and drink with them. Pyle also worried about their safety, urging them to not take chances when they visited the front lines. When he heard that his friend Whitehead planned on going with troops on a risky assignment, Pyle said, "You're a damned fool. Why should you keep on sticking your neck out like that? It's not worth it."

Pyle takes a cigarette break as he inspects the damage to his quarters on the waterfront in Nettuno hit by a German bomb. He told his readers he had not been nervous after the bombing, but did admit to combing his hair with a handkerchief.

There were plenty of dangerous places to be in Italy in early 1944. On January 22, soldiers of the American Fifth Army landed on beaches near the Italian seaside resort towns of Anzio and Nettuno, located about thirty miles south of Rome. Known as Operation Shingle, the amphibious landings were designed to outflank German forces and finally enable Allied troops to capture Rome. Although at first the operation went smoothly, the Germans reacted quickly and soon had American and British soldiers pinned down on the beach under murderous artillery fire.

Pyle failed to take his own advice about correspondents avoiding dangerous assignments and joined American G.I.s at Anzio in late February. When he stepped off the boat and onto the beach, Pyle said he felt like "a clay pigeon in a shooting gallery," as shells exploded within a hundred yards of his position. He wrote Jerry he had planned on staying for only five days, but ended up at Anzio for more than two weeks. "It's pretty dangerous here," he wrote, "but there's a spirit about it that I like better than the other fronts, and my own spirits are better up here."

Although Pyle and other correspondents from America and Great Britain were staying behind the lines in a four-story house in Nettuno, German long-range artillery shells nearly hit the structure on a number of occasions.

Most of the correspondents lived in the bottom floor of the house, considering it to be the safest place to be when the shells started falling. Pyle, however, chose a room on the top floor because it gave him more light to work by in the daytime. "We called it 'Shell Alley' up there because the Anzio-bound shells seemed to come in a groove right past our [window] eaves day and night," he told his readers.

Early in the morning on March 17 Pyle awoke in his room when he heard the sound of American anti-aircraft guns being fired. He had put on his helmet and gone to the window to see what was happening when a terrific blast threw him to the floor. "There was debris flying back and forth all over the room," Pyle remembered. "One gigantic explosion came after another. It was like a great blast of air in which your body felt as light and helpless as a leaf tossed in a whirlwind."

Other correspondents who witnessed the bombing by German planes believed that Pyle had been killed. Wick Fowler of the *Dallas News* turned to George Tucker of the Associated Press and commented, "Well, they got Ernie." They were delighted, however, to learn that the only injury Pyle had received was a cut on his right cheek from flying glass. His fellow correspondents began calling him "Old Indestructible."

ERNIE PYLE STATE HISTORIC SITE

81

Sergeant George Aarons, a photographer for the army magazine *Yank*, discusses the Nettuno bombing with Pyle. Aarons received only a slight wound to his head from the attack.

The close call upset Pyle for a short time. He told Jerry in a letter that the bombing had been "a terrible thing to go through." Although he had planned on leaving Italy for England, he stayed in the Anzio area for an extra week "just purposely to get my nerve back," he wrote Paige Cavanaugh. Pyle finally left Italy on April 5, 1944, and made his way to England, arriving in the middle of the month. He had come to report on the biggest story of the war—the invasion of German-occupied France.

Thousands of American, British, Canadian, and Free French troops were gathered in England preparing to cross the English Channel in landing craft to storm the heavily defended beaches at Normandy in France. Code-named Operation Overlord, the attack, according to British Prime Minister Winston Churchill, would be one of the "most difficult and complicated operations ever to take place."

While in London seeing old friends and preparing for the invasion, Pyle received some good news. Earlier in the year, Miller had received word that the advisory board of Columbia University's Graduate School of Journalism, the group responsible for selecting winners of journalism's highest honor, the Pulitzer Prize, had suggested Pyle's columns on the war be entered for consideration.

Miller sent the columns to the advisory board and also wrote Pyle about

ERNIE PYLE STATE HISTORIC SITE

Pyle talks with soldiers who experienced the fighting in Italy. The conversation was filmed by newsreel cameramen.

what was going on. Pyle expressed his doubts about winning an award, saying his writing "just doesn't fit their rules." A confident Miller bet his friend $100 that Pyle would win the award. In early May Pyle received a phone call from Whitehead congratulating him on winning the Pulitzer Prize for his distinguished war reporting. Pyle wrote Miller that he almost started to cry when he heard the news about capturing the honor. "I didn't realize it meant so much to me," he said. "I never enjoyed losing a bet more."

Of the more than five hundred correspondents in England, twenty-eight, including Pyle, were selected to go with the troops for the initial phase of the Normandy invasion. General Omar Bradley, the commander of the invasion forces and one of Pyle's favorite officers, invited him to observe the operation from his command ship, the USS *Augusta*. On the ship, Pyle could report on the immense operation in relative safety.

Pyle, however, had his own plans. According to Colonel Samuel Myers, an officer Pyle had met in North Africa, the reporter decided there would be "too much brass" aboard the *Augusta*. Pyle decided to "ride with the boys that were going in the hard way," said Myers. On the night of May 31, Pyle boarded the landing ship (LST 353) that would take him and American

American troops face heavy Nazi machine-gun fire as they leave the ramp of a Coast Guard landing boat during the D-Day invasion on June 6, 1944.

soldiers from the First Army from the harbor in Falmouth, England, to their landing site, known by the code name Omaha Beach.

LST 353 was just one of five thousand ships carrying approximately 150,000 Allied troops for the invasion of France. One of the men onboard, Sergeant Arnold Diamondstein, remembered being surprised to see the famous war correspondent step onto the ship's deck. Pyle asked the soldiers to wish him luck, and they all did. "He was . . . our spokesman," Diamondstein wrote his parents. "It was not that his column told us things we did not know or feel, but the fact that we knew you folks at home could read it, and get to know and understand."

On June 6, 1944, the American public heard the words they had been waiting for since the country had entered the war—the landings in France had been a success. The D-Day operation, as it came to be known, had come with a heavy price for the Allied forces. An estimated 2,500 men had lost their lives, and another 7,500 had been wounded or were missing in action. The attack on Omaha Beach had been particularly costly. Protected

A dead American soldier lies facedown in the sand on the beaches of France, one of the many casualties of D-Day. In the background are the obstacles the Germans put in place to defend against the landing.

U.S. NATIONAL ARCHIVES

by fortified bunkers, the Germans had poured down murderous fire on the G.I.s from the First and Twenty-ninth Infantry Divisions as they sprang from their landing craft onto the shore.

The morning after Omaha Beach had been taken and the fighting had moved inland, Pyle spent most of the day walking up and down the beach. In several columns, he described for his readers the destruction left behind after the battle, including burned-out tanks, trucks, and landing craft. "On the beach lay, expended, sufficient men and mechanism for a small war," Pyle said. "They were gone forever now."

For miles along the beach he also saw the "human litter" left behind. "Here are toothbrushes and razors, and snapshots of families back home staring up at you from the sand," Pyle wrote. "Here are pocketbooks, metal mirrors, extra trousers, and bloody, abandoned shoes. Here are broken-handled shovels, and portable radios smashed almost beyond recognition, and mine detectors twisted and ruined."

The swirling tides of the Normandy coast covered and uncovered the bodies of dead soldiers. As Pyle continued to walk he came across what he believed were two pieces of driftwood. "But they weren't driftwood," he said. Instead, they were the feet of a dead soldier sticking up from the sand; the rest of his body had been buried. "The toes of his GI shoes pointed toward the land he had come so far to see," Pyle noted, "and which he saw so briefly."

As Allied troops attempted to break out of the Normandy beachhead against a determined German resistance, Pyle reported on the fighting while visiting such infantry outfits as the First Division, the Twenty-ninth Division, and the Ninth Division. Near the end of June, he went to a press camp set up behind the lines at Vouilly to write about what he had seen. There, he lived in a tent with a group of other correspondents that included Whitehead; Lee; Hank Gorrell, a reporter for United Press; Bert Brandt, a photographer for Acme; and A. J. Liebling, a writer for *New Yorker* magazine.

Every morning, Pyle cooked breakfast—eggs and bacon—on a Coleman stove for Whitehead, Brandt, and himself. "But I'm afraid its popularity is going to devour it," Pyle wrote his wife in early July, "for this morning we had six for breakfast instead of three, and I cook for about an hour before I get everybody fed and get to eat myself." Liebling noted that in addition to other correspondents, soldiers came to visit Pyle, many with complaints they wanted him to hear about and pass along for possible action to high-ranking officers.

COURTESY ANDY ROONEY

Fellow war correspondent Andy Rooney snapped this photograph of Pyle as they reported on the fighting in Normandy.

Joining Pyle at a muddy press camp in Normandy are (left to right) Hal Boyle of the Associated Press, Gordon Gammack of the *Des Moines Register and Tribune*, and Don Whitehead of the Associated Press. While at the camp, Pyle also took time to bathe his feet in his helmet.

Private First Class George Clayton of Evansville shows Pyle an axe he found at a Normandy farm. Clayton served as a Browning Automatic rifleman with the Twenty-ninth Infantry Division and died in combat shortly after this photo was taken. Pyle wrote that Clayton's death "saddened me terribly, for I felt very close to him."

Pyle returned to action in July to witness an attack aimed at breaking the German line near the town of Saint-Lô. The tall, thick hedges that lined the roads in Normandy had slowed the Allied advance to a crawl. In Operation Cobra on July 25, more than a thousand American bombers were ordered to hit the Germans. Once the bombs had stopped falling, U.S. infantry and tanks would attack what enemy was left. If all went well, the road to Paris, France's capital, would be open.

Unfortunately for the G.I.s, the smoke and dust raised by the first wave of bombers caused other Allied planes to drop their bombs short, mistakenly hitting the gathered American troops.

Pyle had been with the Fourth Division when the bombs began falling all around him. He and an officer dove for cover under a wagon. "There is no description of the sound and fury of those bombs," Pyle wrote, "except to say it was chaos, and a waiting for darkness. The feeling of the blast was

Troops of the Twenty-eighth Infantry Division march down the Champs Elysees in Paris on August 29, 1944, freeing the city from Nazi occupation.

sensational. The air struck you in hundreds of continuing flutters. Your ears drummed and rang. You could feel quick little waves of concussions on your chest and in your eyes."

Although Pyle escaped without injury, more than a hundred soldiers were killed and approximately five hundred were wounded. The "friendly fire" disaster, however, did not stop the ground attack from going forward. American forces overwhelmed the shocked German defenders and raced toward Paris. "Anybody makes mistakes," Pyle wrote. "And in this case the percentage of error was really very small compared with the colossal storm of bombs that fell upon the enemy."

The Germans continued to retreat under the constant hammering of Allied infantry and aircraft. On August 25, Pyle found himself with the Second Armored Division of the Free French forces in the newly liberated Paris. Riding in a jeep with Gorrell and two U.S. soldiers, Pyle became surrounded by a cheering crowd of men, women, and children. Despite still hearing the sound of gunfire from other parts of the city, the Parisians wanted to shake the Americans' hands and kiss them. "We all got kissed until we were literally red in [the] face," Pyle said, "and I must say we enjoyed it."

The joy of liberation did little to quiet Pyle's nerves, still raw from enduring the botched bombing raid. He decided, and Miller agreed, that he needed to return home for a rest. "'I've had it,' as they say in the Army," he said in a column titled "Farewell to Europe." After nearly a year near the front lines and writing approximately seven hundred thousand words about the war, Pyle said his spirit had

At the Grand Hotel in Paris, Pyle and Don Whitehead cook rations on a chromium-plated Coleman stove made especially for Pyle by the Coleman company in Wichita, Kansas.

Hal Boyle of the Associated Press, who called himself "the poor man's Pyle," shares one of his articles with Pyle on a balcony of the Grand Hotel in Paris. At the time of this photo, Pyle had grown weary of combat and had decided to return home for a visit.

Pyle's columns had become so popular with American soldiers that the magazine devoted to enlisted men in the service, *Yank*, joked about it on the cover of its October 6, 1944, issue.

Oct. 6, 1944

YANK

THE ARMY WEEKLY

"ERNIE PYLE MISSPELLED HIS NAME."

—Sgt. Al Melinger

grown "wobbly" and his mind "confused." He believed he would go crazy if he heard "one more shot or saw one more dead man."

Soldiers agreed that Pyle needed a rest. Before leaving Paris, Pyle gave an interview to Sergeant Mack Morriss, a correspondent for *Yank*, a magazine printed by the army for its enlisted men. "I figured if I didn't get out pretty soon," Pyle told Morriss, "I'd be a psycho case or something."

As the two men continued to talk, a medic came over to their table and thanked Pyle for his column and said he read it whenever he could. When Pyle replied that he would not be reading it much longer, as he was returning to the United States in a couple of days, the relieved medic said: "Are you? By God, I'm glad. You've seen enough of it. I'm glad you're going."

General Bradley also urged the famed reporter to take a break from the fighting. Bradley even told Pyle he should remain at home for the rest of the war, fearing that he might be wounded or killed if he continued to visit soldiers at the front. However, another war was being waged thousands of miles away in the Pacific. There, American forces were involved in fierce fighting with the Japanese. "It may be that a few months of peace will restore some vim to my spirit," Pyle wrote, "and I can go war-horsing off to the Pacific. We'll see what a little New Mexico sunshine does along that line."

Unfortunately for Pyle, life at home in the fall of 1944 offered little chance for him to get any rest. Everyone, it seemed, wanted the opportunity to see or talk with the famous war correspondent. The families of soldiers still fighting overseas wanted to hear from Pyle about their loved ones. Famous artist Jo Davidson wanted to sculpt a bust of Pyle's head. Both the University of New Mexico and Indiana University offered the reporter honorary doctorate degrees. Lester Cowan, the Hollywood producer responsible for making the movie *The Story of G.I. Joe* based on Pyle's work, arrived with director William Wellman to discuss the film.

LILLY LIBRARY, INDIANA UNIVERSITY

Will Pyle examines a sign placed outside of Dana by the local chapter of the Lions Club honoring the town's famous native son.

During his visit to Indiana University to receive an honorary degree, Pyle visited with his former schoolmates James S. Adams (above, left) and John S. Hastings (above, right); talks with his former *Indiana Daily Student* friend John E. Stempel, who had become chairman of IU's journalism department; and examines an issue of the *Daily Student* with night editor Pat Krieghbaum.

Pyle noted that he worked harder during his "vacation" than he had for most of the time at the front. "Sometimes I feel like sitting down and crying because my old life is gone," he said. His success had made him money and had put his latest book, titled *Brave Men*, which included his columns on the fighting in Sicily, Italy, and France, at the top of the best-seller lists. Being famous, however, made it difficult for him to find time to sit down and talk with old friends. Also, he could no longer go to a restaurant and eat in peace and quiet "because people whisper and stare, and I feel self-conscious," Pyle said.

All the attention and excitement became too much for Jerry to take. She suffered an emotional breakdown, trying to kill herself with a pair of foot-long scissors. Pyle returned from a dental appointment to find Jerry's nurse, Ella Stregar, standing in the yard. "Oh, Ernie," an upset Stregar said, "she's stabbed herself all over." Fortunately, none of Jerry's wounds was life threatening.

Jerry spent time in a hospital near Albuquerque receiving treatment for her injuries, both physical and emotional. When she returned home, Jerry tried to convince Pyle not to cover the fighting in the Pacific. Although very

Pyle joins his wife, Jerry, and the couple's dog, Cheetah, in the living room of their home. Jerry had recently returned home from the hospital after a breakdown.

At his home in Albuquerque, Pyle relaxes with his friend Paige Cavanaugh, who served as an adviser on the film *The Story of G.I. Joe*, which was based on Pyle's work.

On a visit to Hollywood before traveling to the Pacific to report on the war there, Pyle checks a script for *The Story of G.I. Joe* with (left to right) actor Burgess Meredith, who played Pyle in the movie; producer Lester Cowan; and director William Wellman.

worried about going back to the fighting, Pyle decided he needed to return to action. "I'm going simply because there's a war on and I'm part of it," he told his readers, "and I've known all the time I was going back. I'm going simply because I've got to go, and I hate it."

In late December 1944 Jerry went with her husband to California to say goodbye as he left for his new assignment. Before they parted at the railroad station, Pyle gave Jerry a handwritten note that read: "Leaving is brutal for us both, but there'll be a better day, and just keep on keeping yourself for us when I come back. You're wonderful, and doing wonderful. I'm so proud of you."

From the wet jungle of New Guinea to the sandy beaches of Kwajalein and Eniwetok in the Marshall Islands, American troops faced tough opposition from their Japanese foe in the Pacific theater during World War II.

Chapter 7

The Last Assignment

⭐

Okinawa is an island in the Pacific Ocean located just 350 miles from the southern coast of Japan. On Easter Sunday, April 1, 1945, approximately 290,000 Allied troops and 1,500 ships were gathered offshore of Okinawa for what would be the last amphibious landings in the Pacific war. With Operation Iceberg, American military officials hoped to win control of the sixty-mile-long island from its Japanese defenders, the Thirty-second Army. Once Okinawa had been taken, it could serve as the main base for the planned invasion of Japan itself.

Waiting offshore for the invasion with troops of the First Marine Division was Ernie Pyle. For the past few months, Pyle had tried to get used to his new assignment. He compared covering the war in the Pacific to learning how to live in a new city. "The methods of war, the attitude toward it, the homesickness, the distances, the climate—everything is different from what we have known in the European war," he wrote in one column.

One of the big differences between Europe and the Pacific came in the way Americans viewed the enemy. "In Europe we felt our enemies, horrible and deadly as they were, were still people," Pyle said. The fighting between the Japanese and Americans in the Pacific had become a brutal business. Because of the sneak attack on Pearl Harbor and their determination to fight to the death for their leaders, the Japanese were often looked at by American troops "as something inhuman and squirmy," Pyle wrote.

Pyle visits with a B-29 bomber crew at its base on Saipan in the Marianas Islands. Behind Pyle is his relative, Jack Bales, a radar navigator who flew twenty-five combat missions over Japan.

The U.S. Navy had been thrilled to finally have Pyle in the Pacific to offer his readers detailed descriptions of the contributions to the war effort being made by its sailors and airmen. The navy appointed an official escort, Max Miller, to Pyle, and assigned him the best housing at its huge base on the island of Guam. Soldiers and sailors on the base were eager to meet and obtain an autograph from the famous war correspondent. Like others stationed on Pacific islands far from home, the American troops had become bored with the sameness of their lives, "pineapple crazy," as they called it.

As always, Pyle felt uncomfortable about being treated as a celebrity. He missed his home in Albuquerque, New Mexico, and being with the G.I.s he had known in North Africa, Sicily, Italy, and France. Pyle finally found a way to get back into the swing of writing by visiting a bomber base on the nearby island of Saipan. There, he saw a relative, Jack Bales, the step-grandson of Pyle's aunt, Mary Bales. Jack Bales served as a radioman on a B-29, the massive four-engine bomber being used by the air corps to destroy key targets deep inside Japan.

While visiting with Bales and other members of his squadron, Pyle collected material for his column. He also found a comfortable and quiet place to write without any interruptions, turning out seventeen columns in one day. "I'm beginning to get back a little into the swing of working," Pyle wrote his wife. "The first couple of weeks almost killed me; I felt I just never could force myself to write again. And also I seem to have thrown off that awful inner horror of coming back [to the war] that had obsessed me."

After leaving the airmen based on Saipan, Pyle joined the crew of the USS *Cabot*, a small aircraft carrier (known in the navy as a "baby flat-top") whose mission involved bombing sites in Japan and providing support for the landings on the island of Iwo Jima. Although a ship at war, the *Cabot* had onboard five barbers, three doctors, two dentists, two libraries, a laundry, a general store, and a daily newspaper. It seemed to Pyle that the sailors on the ship lived well, as they enjoyed daily baths, good food, and movies every night.

In the three weeks he spent on the *Cabot*, Pyle found it hard to develop the same close relationship with the sailors in the Pacific that he had enjoyed with the soldiers in Europe. Most of the sailors agreed that they had a better life than the G.I.s on the front lines fighting the Nazis. Others, however, were upset at being away from home for long periods. With nothing to look at but water and the occasional lonely island, some sailors even said they would be willing to trade life on a ship for life in a foxhole. "You just have to keep your mouth shut to a remark like that," Pyle wrote in his column.

Pyle returned to Guam to write about his time with the *Cabot*'s crew. On the island, he ran into trouble with navy censors, who wanted to delete all the names of pilots on the aircraft carrier mentioned by Pyle. Of course, one of the reasons he enjoyed such a wide readership was the use of individual soldiers' names. The navy backed down, however, when Pyle threatened to join General Douglas MacArthur's forces fighting the Japanese in the Philippines, or even return to the United States for good.

The battle with the navy censors and his own fear about being back in combat had a bad effect on Pyle's mood. "I'm just now coming out of one of the lowest spells I've ever had," he confessed to his friend Paige Cavanaugh in a March 14, 1945, letter from Guam. "Didn't write a line for five days—just lay on my cot and let my imagination run wild about my own probable personal fate in this war . . . and got lower and lower." Pyle did return to writing, but found it to be a struggle to complete his work to his satisfaction.

When news came of the planned invasion of Okinawa, Pyle at first expressed great reluctance at covering the operation. According to Miller, Pyle spent three sleepless nights debating whether or not he should report on the battle for his readership, which had grown to four hundred daily and three hundred weekly newspapers. He believed he would be killed if he went in with the troops for the landings.

On the fourth day of his debate, Pyle decided to go. "Now I feel all right again," Pyle told Miller. "I think I'll come through it after all." As he prepared to sail on an assault transport ship with troops from the First Marine Division, Pyle and other reporters were told by navy officers to be prepared for fierce opposition from the more than 100,000 Japanese soldiers defending Okinawa. After the briefing, Pyle turned to another reporter and said, "What I need now is a great big drink."

Pyle prepared for the ordeal ahead of him by getting as much sleep as he could in a room he shared with U.S. Marine Major Reed Taylor, a veteran of the fighting on the island of Guadalcanal earlier in the war. Between his naps, Pyle tried to catch up on his reading and listened to the latest war news broadcast once or twice a day over the ship's loudspeakers. "Every little bit of good news cheers us," he noted. "The ship, of course, is full of rumors, good and bad, but nobody believes any of them."

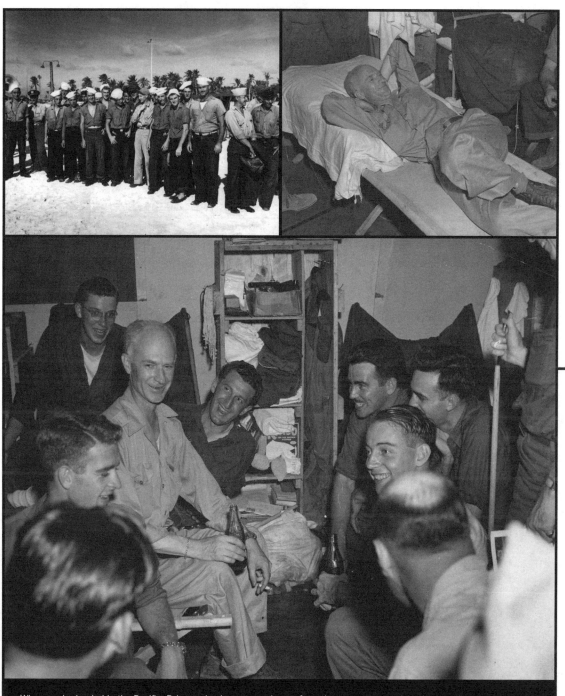

Wherever he landed in the Pacific, Pyle received a warm welcome from the navy, army, and marines stationed on the island bases. He listened to their stories, drank soft drinks with them, and also rested when he could.

On the morning of the Okinawa invasion, Pyle enjoyed a ham-and-egg breakfast before stepping into a landing craft for his trip to shore with the Fifth Marine Regiment. He and other correspondents were set to land about an hour and a half after the American forces first hit the beach. "There's nothing romantic whatever in knowing that an hour from now you may be dead," Pyle wrote. He also dreaded what he might find on the beach—the mangled bodies of wounded and dead marines he had come to know well on the voyage.

Both Pyle and the marines were delighted to learn there had been very few casualties; the landings had been unopposed by the Japanese. One of the relieved marines said he wished he could "wear Ernie Pyle around his neck as a good-luck charm" for the rest of the war. The beach was quiet enough for Pyle to enjoy a picnic meal of turkey wings, bread, oranges, and apples. "You can't know the relief I felt," he wrote his wife after the invasion, "for as you know I had dreaded this one terribly. Now it is behind me, and I will never make another landing, so I can't help but feel good about that."

The ease of the initial landings on Okinawa gave way to much tougher

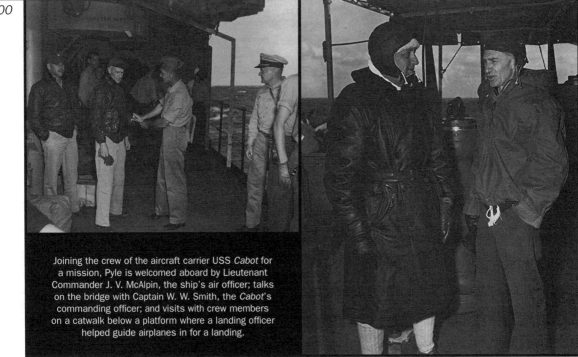

Joining the crew of the aircraft carrier USS *Cabot* for a mission, Pyle is welcomed aboard by Lieutenant Commander J. V. McAlpin, the ship's air officer; talks on the bridge with Captain W. W. Smith, the *Cabot*'s commanding officer; and visits with crew members on a catwalk below a platform where a landing officer helped guide airplanes in for a landing.

fighting as American troops made their way inland. The main Japanese force had withdrawn to the southern portion of the island. There the enemy hid their artillery and heavy weapons in caves and dugouts, protecting them from attacks from the air and from ships offshore. Japanese kamikaze pilots deliberately crashed their aircraft into the ships of the American navy, sinking more than thirty of them. Both sides suffered tremendous casualties as the fighting continued until the end of June.

Pyle spent two days with the marines before returning to his ship to write. He rejoined the Fifth Marine Regiment and was on hand when they captured some frightened Japanese soldiers. "Fortunately they happened to be the surrendering kind, rather than [the] fight-to-death kind, or they could have killed several of us," Pyle wrote Jerry of the experience. "They were the first Jap soldiers I'd ever seen in the raw before capture."

On the evening of April 7 Pyle left Okinawa and went aboard the USS *Panamint*, the command ship for the invasion, to write and recover from a cold he had caught. On board he shared quarters with another correspondent, Robert Sherrod, author of a best-selling book on the bloody invasion of Tarawa in the Pacific.

Sherrod told Pyle he had decided to return to the United States after a few more days, and Pyle indicated he had also grown tired of war. "I'm getting too old to stay in combat with these kids," Pyle said, "and I'm going to go home, too, in about a month."

While on the *Panamint*, however, Pyle learned about another operation, involving the Seventy-seventh Infantry Division, to capture Ie Shima, a ten-mile-square island located west of Okinawa and home to three Japanese airfields. The operation was set for April 16. Pyle agreed to go with the troops for the fight, but only after the initial landing had been made. "I've got almost a spooky feeling that I've been spared once more and that it would be asking for it to tempt Fate again," he wrote Miller. "So I'm going to keep my promise to you and to myself that that [Okinawa] was the last one. I'll be on operations in the future, of course, but not on any more landings."

As the correspondent prepared to cover another battle, he heard on April 12 of the death of President Franklin D. Roosevelt. The news came as

On the way to view the invasion of Okinawa, Pyle is entertained on a transport ship by Private First Class Johnny Marturello from Des Moines, Iowa. In addition, Pyle autographs a marine's cap and listens to a news broadcast with members of the transport's crew.

a shock to Pyle and American forces around the world. "The war will go on just the same," Pyle wrote his relatives in Dana, Indiana, "but I don't know of anyone with the knowledge and strength to help arrange the peace."

The Seventy-seventh Infantry Division met with stiff resistance from the Japanese on Ie Shima when it hit the beach on April 16—a landing Pyle observed from the *Panamint*. "Not one Jap soldier surrendered," said one soldier. "He killed until he was killed." Japanese troops remained hidden in dugouts and foxholes, letting the Americans pass by before springing out of their hiding places to fire at them. Some of the enemy strapped explosives to their backs and blew themselves up under tanks or where groups of G.I.s had gathered.

On April 17 Pyle and other correspondents climbed aboard a landing craft for a trip to Ie Shima's beach. After landing, Pyle went to the command post of the division's 305th Regiment. As he talked to the soldiers and their officers, Pyle saw one G.I. killed by a Japanese mine. "I wish I was in Albuquerque!" he exclaimed. He spent the night on Ie Shima, sleeping in a former Japanese dugout.

Pyle (third from left) joins members of the First Marine Division during the invasion of Okinawa. The tired correspondent also takes a break from the action with Private First Class Urban Vachon of Laconia, New Hampshire. Pyle compared Vachon to the tired soldiers of Europe drawn by his friend, cartoonist Bill Mauldin.

ERNIE PYLE STATE HISTORIC SITE

During his time on Okinawa, Pyle had the services of a driver, Private First Class J. P. Murray of Winthrop, Massachusetts.

At about ten o'clock the next morning, Pyle climbed into a jeep with Lieutenant Colonel Joseph B. Coolidge, commanding officer of the 305th Regiment. Coolidge and three other soldiers were hoping to find a site for a new command post for the regiment.

Joining Pyle and Coolidge on the trip were Major George H. Pratt and two enlisted men, Dale W. Bassett and John L. Barnes. They traveled down a narrow road that had been cleared of mines and appeared to be safe. "We followed some 2½ ton trucks and every indication pointed to a fairly calm trip except for occasional mortars dropping into the open fields on either hand," said Coolidge.

As the jeep slowed to avoid the traffic ahead near the village of Ie, a

Japanese soldier hidden in a coral ridge about a third of a mile away fired on the vehicle with his Nambu machine gun. "All of us without a second thought jumped for safety into the ditch on either side of the road," Coolidge said. Pyle, Bassett, and Coolidge dove into a ditch on the right-hand side of the road, while Barnes went to the left and Pratt crouched further ahead in a ditch near a small farm road.

Both Coolidge and Pyle raised their heads to see if the others had been hit by the enemy's fire. "The Jap then let go at us again—he had had time to adjust his sights on the two of us," said Coolidge. After ducking the bullets, the officer turned to see Pyle lying on the ground with blood flowing from a hit to his left temple. America's favorite war correspondent was dead.

After recovering Pyle's body, soldiers built a coffin for their friend and buried him along with others killed on Ie Shima. About two hundred men from all ranks and representing all parts of the armed forces attended the burial service held on April 20. "With the exception of an occasional blast of distant guns and the murmuring of the waves 100 yards away, all was quiet," recalled Nathaniel B. Saucier, the 305th Regiment's chaplain.

Pyle's wife Jerry learned of her husband's death at her home in Albuquerque before it was released

An aerial view of Ie Shima, with the mountain Iegusugu Yama in the background.

to the press. In Dana, a neighbor heard about Pyle's death on a radio news broadcast and brought the grim news to the reporter's father and aunt. When he learned that his son had been killed, Will Pyle broke down in tears. Messages of sympathy came from the new president, Harry Truman, and soldiers who had known Pyle. "The GIs in Europe—and that means all of us here—have lost one of our best and most understanding friends," noted General Dwight D. Eisenhower.

On May 7, 1945, nearly a week after Adolf Hitler committed suicide in his Berlin bunker, officials representing the German government signed documents at a schoolhouse in Reims, France, unconditionally surrendering to the Allied forces, effective May 8. Victory in Europe had been achieved. Before his death, Pyle had written a column to be released when the war in

Chaplain Nathaniel B. Saucier offers a few words of prayer before Pyle's coffin on Ie Shima. Because fighting continued on the island, those attending the service were required to wear their helmets and carry their weapons with them.

Field Marshall Wilhelm Keitel signs the ratified surrender terms for the German army on May 7, 1945.

Europe finally ended. In it, he said the column was his way of honoring the men who had been his friends throughout the fighting in North Africa, Sicily, Italy, and France. "My one great regret of the war," he said, "is that I am not with them when it has ended."

The war in the Pacific continued after the surrender of Germany. On August 6, a B-29 bomber nicknamed the *Enola Gay* dropped a new weapon, the atomic bomb, on the Japanese city of Hiroshima. The resulting explosion of just one bomb leveled the city and killed thousands of

Rain-soaked Indianapolis residents celebrate the announcement that Japan had offered its unconditional surrender to Allied forces in the Pacific.

Japanese soldiers and civilians. Three days later, a second atomic bomb destroyed the city of Nagasaki. On August 15 the Japanese emperor, Hirohito, announced in a radio broadcast to his people that the country was surrendering. World War II had ended.

Jerry Pyle lived long enough to accept from the U.S. government a Medal of Merit for her husband's work in the war. Still grieving his loss, she died on November 23, 1945. Four years after the war's end, military officials moved Ernie Pyle's body to the National Memorial Cemetery of the Pacific, Punchbowl Crater, Oahu, Hawaii.

In the years since Pyle's death there have been numerous wars involving American soldiers. Newspaper reporters, radio broadcasters, and television newsmen have done their best to give an accurate and realistic view of combat to people back home. Nobody, however, has come close to the popularity and respect enjoyed by Pyle from civilians and soldiers alike.

While he covered the war in the Pacific, Pyle sent a copy of his book *Brave Men* to General Eisenhower. The commander of Allied forces in the fight against Nazi Germany wrote the reporter to thank him for the book and to volunteer to help Pyle spread the word about the sacrifices being made by the infantry on behalf of democracy.

Pyle wrote Eisenhower in late February 1945 that perhaps they were "both fighting a losing cause," as no matter how much was written about combat, those who had never experienced war could never fully understand what it had been like. In "carrying the torch" for the foot soldier for more than two-and-a-half years, Pyle said he tried to make people back home care about the G.I., but he had not been able to make them really feel what a soldier went through during battle. "I believe it's impossible," wrote Pyle. "But I'll keep on trying."

An honor guard prepares to lay to rest Pyle's body in ceremonies at the National Memorial Cemetery of the Pacific, Punchbowl Crater, Oahu, Hawaii, on July 19, 1949.

World War II Columns by Pyle

Reprinted by permission of the Scripps-Howard Foundation

★

The God-Damned Infantry
May 2, 1943

We're now with an infantry outfit that has battled ceaselessly for four days and nights.

This northern warfare has been in the mountains. You don't ride much anymore. It is walking and climbing and crawling country. The mountains aren't big, but they are constant. They are largely treeless. They are easy to defend and bitter to take. But we are taking them.

The Germans lie on the back slope of every ridge, deeply dug into foxholes. In front of them the fields and pastures are hideous with thousands of hidden mines. The forward slopes are left open, untenanted, and if the Americans tried to scale these slopes they would be murdered wholesale in an inferno of machine-gun crossfire plus mortars and grenades.

Consequently we don't do it that way. We have fallen back to the old warfare of first pulverizing the enemy with artillery, then sweeping around the ends of the hill with infantry and taking them from the sides and behind.

* * *

I've written before how the big guns crack and roar almost constantly throughout the day and night. They lay a screen ahead of our troops. By magnificent shooting they drop shells on the back slopes. By means of shells timed to burst in the air a few feet from the ground, they get the Germans even in their foxholes. Our troops have found that the Germans dig foxholes down and then under, trying to get cover from the shell bursts that shower death from above.

Our artillery has really been sensational. For once we have enough of something and at the right time. Officers tell me they actually have more guns than they know what to do with.

All the guns in any one sector can be centered to shoot at one spot. And when we lay the whole business on a German hill the whole slope seems to erupt. It becomes an unbelievable cauldron of fire and smoke and dirt. Veteran German soldiers say they have never been through anything like it.

* * *

Now to the infantry—the God-damned infantry, as they like to call themselves.

I love the infantry because they are the underdogs. They are the mud-rain-frost-and-wind boys. They have no comforts, and they even learn to live without the necessities. And in the end they are the guys that wars can't be won without.

I wish you could see just one of the ineradicable pictures I have in my mind today. In this particular picture I am sitting among clumps of sword-grass on a steep and rocky hillside that we have just taken. We are looking out over a vast rolling country to the rear.

A narrow path comes like a ribbon over a hill miles away, down a long slope, across a creek, up a slope and over another hill.

All along the length of this ribbon there is now a thin line of men. For four days and nights they have fought hard, eaten little, washed none, and slept hardly at all. Their nights have been violent with attack, fright, butchery, and their days sleepless and miserable with the crash of artillery.

The men are walking. They are fifty feet apart, for dispersal. Their walk is slow, for they are dead weary, as you can tell even when looking at them from behind. Every line and sag of their bodies speaks their inhuman exhaustion.

On their shoulders and backs they carry heavy steel tripods, machine-gun barrels, leaden boxes of ammunition. Their feet seem to sink into the ground from the overload they are bearing.

They don't slouch. It is the terrible deliberation of each step that spells out their appalling tiredness. Their faces are black and unshaven. They are young men, but the grime and whiskers and exhaustion make them look middle-aged.

In their eyes as they pass is not hatred, not excitement, not despair, not the tonic of their victory—there is just the simple expression of being here as though they had been here doing this forever, and nothing else.

The line moves on, but it never ends. All afternoon men keep coming round the hill and vanishing eventually over the horizon. It is one long tired line of antlike men.

* * *

There is an agony in your heart and you almost feel ashamed to look at them. They are just guys from Broadway and Main Street, but you wouldn't remember them. They are too far away now. They are too tired. Their world can never be known to you, but if you could see them just once, just for an instant, you would know that no matter how hard people work back home they are not keeping pace with these infantrymen in Tunisia.

The Death of Captain Waskow
January 10, 1944

In this war I have known a lot of officers who were loved and respected by the soldiers under them. But never have I crossed the trail of any man as beloved as Capt. Henry T. Waskow of Belton, Texas.

Capt. Waskow was a company commander in the 36th Division. He had led his company since long before it left the States. He was very young, only in his middle twenties, but he carried in him a sincerity and gentleness that made people want to be guided by him.

"After my own father, he came next," a sergeant told me.

"He always looked after us," a soldier said. "He'd go to bat for us every time."

"I've never knowed him to do anything unfair," another one said.

I was at the foot of the mule trail the night they brought Capt. Waskow's body down. The moon was nearly full at the time, and you could see far up the trail, and even part way across the valley below. Soldiers made shadows in the moonlight as they walked.

Dead men had been coming down the mountain all evening, lashed onto the backs of mules. They came lying belly-down across the wooden pack-saddles, their heads hanging down on the left side of the mule, their stiffened legs sticking out awkwardly from the other side, bobbing up and down as the mule walked.

The Italian mule-skinners were afraid to walk beside dead men, so Americans had to lead the mules down that night. Even the Americans were reluctant to unlash and lift off the bodies at the bottom, so an officer had to do it himself, and ask others to help.

The first one came early in the morning. They slid him down from the mule and stood him on his feet for a moment, while they got a new grip. In the half light he might have been merely a sick man standing there, leaning on the others. Then they laid him on the ground in the shadow of the low stone wall alongside the road.

I don't know who that first one was. You feel small in the presence of dead men, and ashamed at being alive, and you don't ask silly questions.

We left him there beside the road, that first one, and we all went back into the cowshed and sat on water cans or lay on the straw, waiting for the next batch of mules.

Somebody said the dead soldier had been dead for four days, and then nobody said anything more about it. We talked soldier talk for an hour or more. The dead man lay all alone outside in the shadow of the low stone wall.

Then a soldier came into the cowshed and said there were some more bodies outside. We went out into the road. Four mules stood there, in the moonlight, in the road where the trail came down off the mountain. The soldiers who led them stood there waiting. "This one is Captain Waskow," one of them said quietly.

Two men unlashed his body from the mule and lifted it off and laid it in the shadow beside the low stone wall. Other men took the other bodies off. Finally there were five lying end to end in a long row, alongside the road. You don't cover up dead men in the combat zone. They just lie there in the shadows until somebody else comes after them.

The unburdened mules moved off to their olive orchard. The men in the road seemed reluctant to leave. They stood around, and gradually one by one I could sense them moving close to Capt. Waskow's body. Not so much to look, I think, as to say something in finality to him, and to themselves. I stood close by and I could hear.

One soldier came and looked down, and he said out loud, "God damn it." That's all he said, and then he walked away. Another one came. He said, "God damn it to hell anyway." He looked down for a few last moments, and then he turned and left.

Another man came; I think he was an officer. It was hard to tell officers from men in the half light, for all were bearded and grimy dirty. The man looked down into the dead captain's face, and then he spoke directly to him, as though he were alive. He said: "I'm sorry, old man."

Then a soldier came and stood beside the officer, and bent over, and he too spoke to his dead captain, not in a whisper but awfully tenderly, and he said:

"I sure am sorry, sir."

Then the first man squatted down, and he reached down and took the dead hand, and he sat there for a full five minutes, holding the dead hand in his own and looking intently into the dead face, and he never uttered a sound all the time he sat there.

And finally he put the hand down, and then reached up and gently straightened the points of the captain's shirt collar, and then he sort of re-arranged the tattered edges of his uniform around the wound. And then he got up and walked away down the road in the moonlight, all alone.

After that the rest of us went back into the cowshed, leaving the five dead men lying in a line, end to end, in the shadow of the low stone wall. We lay down on the straw in the cowshed, and pretty soon we were all asleep.

The Horrible Waste of War
June 16, 1944

I took a walk along the historic coast of Normandy in the country of France.

It was a lovely day for strolling along the seashore. Men were sleeping on the sand, some of them sleeping forever. Men were floating in the water, but they didn't know they were in the water, for they were dead.

The water was full of squishy little jellyfish about the size of your hand.

Millions of them. In the center each of them had a green design exactly like a four-leaf clover. The good-luck emblem. Sure. Hell yes.

I walked for a mile and a half along the water's edge of our many-miled invasion beach. You wanted to walk slowly, for the detail on that beach was infinite.

The wreckage was vast and startling. The awful waste and destruction of war, even aside from the loss of human life, has always been one of its outstanding features to those who are in it. Anything and everything is expendable. And we did expend on our beachhead in Normandy during those first few hours.

* * *

For a mile out from the beach there were scores of tanks and trucks and boats that you could no longer see, for they were at the bottom of the water—swamped by overloading, or hit by shells, or sunk by mines. Most of their crews were lost.

You could see trucks tipped half over and swamped. You could see partly sunken barges, and the angled-up corners of jeeps, and small landing craft half submerged. And at low tide you could still see those vicious six-pronged iron snares that helped snag and wreck them.

On the beach itself, high and dry, were all kinds of wrecked vehicles. There were tanks that had only just made the beach before being knocked out. There were jeeps that had been burned to a dull gray. There were big derricks on caterpillar treads that didn't quite make it. There were half-tracks carrying office equipment that had been made into a shambles by a single shell hit, their interiors still holding their useless equipage of smashed typewriters, telephones, office files.

There were LCT's turned completely upside down, and lying on their backs, and how they got that way I don't know. There were boats stacked on top of each other, their sides caved in, their suspension doors knocked off.

In this shoreline museum of carnage there were abandoned rolls of barbed wire and smashed bulldozers and big stacks of thrown-away lifebelts and piles of shells still waiting to be moved.

In the water floated empty life rafts and soldiers' packs and ration boxes, and mysterious oranges.

On the beach lay snarled rolls of telephone wire and big rolls of steel matting and stacks of broken, rusting rifles.

On the beach lay, expended, sufficient men and mechanism for a small war. They were gone forever now. And yet we could afford it.

We could afford it because we were on, we had our toehold, and behind us there were such enormous replacements for this wreckage on the beach that you could hardly conceive of their sum total. Men and equipment were flowing from England in such a gigantic stream that it made the waste on the beachhead seem like nothing at all, really nothing at all.

* * *

A few hundred yards back on the beach is a high bluff. Up there we had a tent hospital, and a barbed-wire enclosure for prisoners of war. From up there you could see far up and down the beach, in a spectacular crow's-nest view, and far out to sea.

And standing out there on the water beyond all this wreckage was the greatest armada man has ever seen. You simply could not believe the gigantic collection of ships that lay out there waiting to unload.

Looking from the bluff, it lay thick and clear to the far horizon of the sea and beyond, and it spread out to the sides and was miles wide. Its utter enormity would move the hardest man.

As I stood up there I noticed a group of freshly taken German prisoners standing nearby. They had not yet been put in the prison cage. They were just standing there, a couple of doughboys leisurely guarding them with tommy guns.

The prisoners too were looking out to sea—the same bit of sea that for months and years had been so safely empty before their gaze. Now they stood staring almost as if in a trance.

They didn't say a word to each other. They didn't need to. The expression on their faces was something forever unforgettable. In it was the final horrified acceptance of their doom.

If only all Germans could have had the rich experience of standing on the bluff and looking out across the water and seeing what their compatriots saw.

On Victory in Europe
(The following is a draft of a column Pyle wrote, but never published, about the end of the war in Europe.)

And so it is over. The catastrophe on one side of the world has run its course. The day that it had so long seemed would never come has come at last.

I suppose emotions here in the Pacific are the same as they were among the Allies all over the world. First a shouting of the good news with such joyous surprise that you would think the shouter himself had brought it about.

And then an unspoken sense of gigantic relief—and then a hope that the collapse in Europe would hasten the end in the Pacific.

It has been seven months since I heard my last shot in the European war. Now I am as far away from it as it is possible to get on this globe.

This is written on a little ship lying off the coast of the Island of Okinawa, just south of Japan, on the other side of the world from Ardennes.

But my heart is still in Europe, and that's why I am writing this column.

It is to the boys who were my friends for so long. My one regret of the war is that I was not with them when it ended.

For the companionship of two and a half years of death and misery is a spouse that tolerates no divorce. Such companionship finally becomes a part of one's soul, and it cannot be obliterated.

True, I am with American boys in the other war not yet ended, but I am old-fashioned and my sentiment runs to old things.

To me the European war is old, and the Pacific war is new.

Last summer I wrote that I hoped the end of the war could be a gigantic relief, but not an elation. In the joyousness of high spirits it is easy for us to forget the dead. Those who are gone would not wish themselves to be a millstone of gloom around our necks.

But there are many of the living who have had burned into their brains forever the unnatural sight of cold dead men scattered over the hillsides and in the ditches along the high rows of hedge throughout the world.

Dead men by mass production—in one country after another—month after month and year after year. Dead men in winter and dead men in summer.

Dead men in such familiar promiscuity that they become monotonous.

Dead men in such monstrous infinity that you come almost to hate them.

These are the things that you at home need not even try to understand. To you at home they are columns of figures, or he is a near one who went away and just didn't come back. You didn't see him lying so grotesque and pasty beside the gravel road in France.

We saw him, saw him by the multiple thousands. That's the difference. . . .

Learn More about Pyle

★

After his death in 1945, Ernie Pyle left behind a wealth of material about his life as a roving reporter in the United States and as a war correspondent during World War II. The Lilly Library at Indiana University in Bloomington, Indiana, has a number of collections involving Pyle's life, including letters to his wife, Jerry; to his mother, father, and aunt in Dana, Indiana; and to his friend Paige Cavanaugh. The library also has Pyle's columns and newspaper articles and other materials about his life.

The Ernie Pyle State Historic Site in Dana, Indiana, has the papers of Lee Graham Miller, Pyle's friend and editor for many years. The collection includes letters to and from Miller and Pyle, as well as information from other sources gathered by Miller for his biography of Pyle. The book, *The Story of Ernie Pyle*, was published by the Viking Press of New York in 1950. Miller also produced a photo biography of Pyle titled *An Ernie*

Pyle Album: Indiana to Ie Shima (New York: William Sloane Associates, 1946).

The Indiana Historical Society's William Henry Smith Memorial Library in Indianapolis, Indiana, is home to the private library of Pyle and his wife. The collection of 350 books, formerly located at the Indiana University School of Journalism, includes review copies of books sent to Pyle by other authors, travel books he used during his days as a roving correspondent, and classic works by such notable writers as Mark Twain and H. G. Wells.

The most recent and complete biography of Pyle is James Tobin's *Ernie Pyle's War: America's Eyewitness to World War II* (New York: Free Press, 1997). David Nichols has produced two collections of Pyle's works, both of which include biographical essays. These books are *Ernie's War: The Best of Ernie Pyle's World War II Dispatches* (New York: Random House, 1986) and *Ernie's America: The Best of Ernie Pyle's 1930s Travel Dispatches* (New York: Random House, 1989). A selection of Pyle's aviation columns appears in Mike Harden and Evelyn Hobson's *On a Wing and a Prayer: The Aviation Columns of Ernie Pyle* (Dana, IN: Friends of Ernie Pyle, 1995).

A number of collections of Pyle's columns were published during and after his lifetime. These included his war works: *Ernie Pyle in England* (New York: Robert McBride, 1941); *Here Is Your War* (New York: Henry Holt, 1943); *Brave Men* (New York: Henry Holt, 1944); and *Last Chapter* (New York: Henry Holt, 1946). A selection of his travel columns appeared in the book *Home Country* (New York: William Sloane, 1947). Some of Pyle's best-known World War II columns are also included in *Reporting World War II, Parts One and Two* (New York: Library of America, 1995).

A number of articles and books also cover Pyle and his career and the United States's role in World War II in Europe and in the Pacific. These include the following:

Ruth Padget Albright, "Ernie Pyle at Indiana University," *Traces of Indiana and Midwestern History* (Spring 2000).

Stephen E. Ambrose, *D-Day, June 6, 1944: The Climactic Battle of World War II* (New York: Simon & Schuster, 1994).

———, *The Good Fight: How World War II Was Won* (New York: Atheneum Books for Young Readers, 2001).

Rick Atkinson, *An Army at Dawn: The War in North Africa, 1942–1943* (New York: Henry Holt and Co., 2002).

Bob Bales, *Ernie Pyle: A Hoosier Childhood* (n.p.: The Rivendell Book Factory, 2002). [A fictionalized account of the reporter's youth in Dana written by a Pyle relative.]

John Morton Blum, *V Was for Victory: Politics and American Culture during World War II* (New York: Harcourt Brace Jovanovich, 1976).

Ray E. Boomhower, *"One Shot": The World War II Photography of John A. Bushemi* (Indianapolis: Indiana Historical Society Press, 2004).

Tom Brokaw, *The Greatest Generation* (New York: Random House, 1998).

John Ellis, *The Sharp End: The Fighting Man in World War II* (New York: Charles Scribner's Sons, 1980).

"Ernie Pyle's War," *Time*, July 17, 1944.

Rudy Faircloth, *"Buddy" Ernie Pyle: World War II's Most Beloved Typewriter Soldier* (Tabor City, NC: Atlantic Publishing, 1982).

Paul Fussell, *The Boys' Crusade: The American Infantry in Northwestern Europe, 1944–1945* (New York: Modern Library, 2003).

————, *Wartime: Understanding and Behavior in the Second World War* (New York: Oxford University Press, 1989).

Martin Gilbert, *D-Day* (Hoboken, NJ: John Wiley & Sons, 2004).

Lee Kennett, *G.I.: The American Soldier in World War II* (New York: Charles Scribner's Sons, 1987).

A. J. Liebling, "Pyle Set the Style," *New Yorker*, September 2, 1950.

Gerald F. Linderman, *The World Within War: America's Combat Experience in World War II* (New York: Free Press, 1997).

Richard R. Lingeman, *Don't You Know There's a War On? The American Home Front, 1941–1945* (New York: G. P. Putnam's Sons, 1970).

John C. McManus, *The Deadly Brotherhood: The American Combat Soldier in World War II* (Novato, CA: Presidio Press, 1998).

Richard Melzer, *Ernie Pyle in the American Southwest* (Sante Fe, NM: Sunstone Press, 1995).

Barbara O'Connor, *The Soldiers' Voice: The Story of Ernie Pyle* (Minneapolis, MN: Carolrhoda Books, Inc., 1996).

Frederick C. Painton, "The Hoosier Letter-Writer," in *More Post Biographies* (Athens: University of Georgia Press, 1947).

Andrew A. Rooney, *My War* (New York: Times Books, 1995).

Steve Sanders, "Hoosier Vagabond: Ernie Pyle, 1900–1945," *Indiana Alumni Magazine* (July/August 1985).

David Smurthwaite, *The Pacific War Atlas, 1941–1945* (New York: Facts on File, 1995).

Ronald H. Spector, *Eagle against the Sun: The American War with Japan* (New York: Free Press, 1985).

Michael S. Sweeney, "Appointment at Hill 1205: Ernie Pyle and Captain Henry T. Waskow," http://www.kwanah.com/txmilmus/36division/sweeney.htm.

Frederick Voss, *Reporting the War: The Journalistic Coverage of World War II* (Washington, DC: Smithsonian Institution Press, 1994).

World War II Web Sites

"A People at War"
National Archives and Records Administration
http://www.archives.gov/exhibits/a_people_at_war/a_people_at_war.html

The Air Force Historical Research Agency
http://www.au.af.mil/au/afhra/

The Avalon Project at Yale Law School: World War II Documents
http://www.yale.edu/lawweb/avalon/wwii/wwii.htm

British Broadcasting Corporation Online: World War II
http://www.bbc.co.uk/history/war/wwtwo/index.shtml

National World War II Memorial
http://www.wwiimemorial.com/

The National D-Day Museum
http://www.ddaymuseum.org/

The National Museum of the Pacific War
http://www.nimitz-museum.org/

The Naval Historical Center
http://www.history.navy.mil/

U.S. Army Center of Military History
http://www.army.mil/cmh-pg/

USS *Arizona* Memorial
http://www.nps.gov/usar/

World War II Resources
http://www.ibiblio.org/pha/

Yahoo World War II Index
http://dir.yahoo.com/Arts/Humanities/History/By_Time_Period/20th_Century/Military_History/World_War_II/

An exterior and interior view of the Ernie Pyle State Historic Site in Dana, Indiana.

Pyle Historic Sites

★

The following historic sites will lead the reader to a broader understanding of some of the most important experiences in Ernie Pyle's life. If you plan on making a visit to one of these places, please call, write, or visit their Web sites for the most up-to-date information.

The **Ernie Pyle State Historic Site** is located in Pyle's hometown of Dana, Indiana. The museum is operated by the Indiana State Museum System. Through the efforts of the Indiana Department of the American Legion and financial support from the Eli Lilly Foundation, Pyle's birthplace home was moved from its rural site to its present location. It became a state historic site in July 1976.

On April 18, 1995, the site dedicated a new Visitor Center, constructed from two authentic World War II Quonset huts. The center features a video theater, research library, exhibitions, and a gift shop. The Scripps-Howard Foundation gave a generous donation for the building of the Visitor Center. Support also came from the estate of Paige Cavanaugh.

Admission to the site, which is located one mile north of US 36 on Indiana 71, is free. The Ernie Pyle State Historic Site is open from 9 a.m. to 5 p.m. Thursday through Saturday, and 1 p.m. to 5 p.m. on Sunday, from April 1 through November. For more information and hours of operation, call the museum at (765) 665-9312 or visit its Web site at http://www.in.gov/ism/HistoricSites/ErniePyle/Historic.asp.

Since 1948, the former **Ernie Pyle Home** at 900 Girard SE in Albuquerque, New Mexico, has served as a branch library of the Albuquerque/Bernalillo County Library System. The City of Albuquerque purchased the home of the famous war correspondent and his wife Jerry from the Pyle estate. The Pyle library features memorabilia from Pyle's life. The library's hours are from 10 a.m. to 6 p.m. Tuesday, Thursday, Friday, and Saturday, and from 11 a.m. to 7 p.m. on Wednesdays. For more information, contact the Pyle library at (505) 256-2065, or visit the Albuquerque/Bernalillo County Library System's Web site at http://www.cabq.gov/library/.

Index

131